JOURNEY
THROUGH THE
BIBLE

KEN WADE

Other books by Ken Wade

Del Delker
Journey to Moriah
The Orion Conspiracy
Paul: A Spiritual Journey

By Don Schneider with Ken Wade

Really Living
Really Living 2

JOURNEY THROUGH THE BIBLE

KEN WADE

The Voice of Prophecy

FROM GENESIS TO JOB

Pacific Press® Publishing Association
Nampa, Idaho
Oshawa, Ontario, Canada
www.pacificpress.com

Cover design by Gerald Lee Monks
Cover resources from iStockphoto.com and dreamstime.com
Inside design by Kristin Hansen-Mellish

The author assumes full responsibility for the accuracy of all facts and quotations as cited in this book.

Scriptures quoted from Jerusalem are from *The Jerusalem Bible,* copyright © 1966 by Darton, Longman & Todd, Ltd., and Doubleday & Company, Inc. Used by permission of the publisher.

Scriptures quoted from NEB are from *The New English Bible,* copyright © The Delegates of the Oxford University Press and the Syndics of the Cambridge University Press 1961, 1970. Reprinted by permission.

Scriptures quoted from NIV are from THE HOLY BIBLE, NEW INTERNATIONAL VERSION®, NIV®. Copyright © 1973, 1978, 1984, 2011 by Biblica, Inc.™ Used by permission. All rights reserved worldwide.

Scriptures quoted from NKJV are from The New King James Version, copyright © 1979, 1980, 1982, Thomas Nelson, Inc., Publishers.

Scriptures quoted from NRSV are from the New Revised Standard Version of the Bible, copyright © 1989 by the Division of Christian Education of the National Council of the Churches of Christ in the U.S.A. Used by permission. All rights reserved.

Scriptures quoted from Phillips are from J. B. Phillips: The New Testament in Modern English, Revised Edition, copyright © J. B. Phillips 1958, 1960, 1972. Used by permission of Macmillan Publishing Co., Inc.

Additional copies of this book may be obtained by calling toll-free 1-800-765-6955 or online at www.adventistbookcenter.com.

ISBN 13: 978-0-8136-4309-6
ISBN 10: 0-8163-4309-8

13 14 15 16 17 • 5 4 3 2 1

Contents

Preface

When at the beginning of the year 2000 our Voice of Prophecy staff decided to begin a journey through the entire Bible, preparing radio broadcasts focusing on each book individually, I had no idea what a great adventure we had embarked upon.

Our journey through the Bible, along with other programs focusing specifically on the Gospels, filled most of the next three years of my life. It gave me the opportunity to study the Book of books in greater depth than I ever had before.

There had been times during my ministry when I had challenged myself to read the Bible through in a year. One year I actually made it through by the middle of May; most years, I got bogged down and never finished.

Now I assigned myself to read each book of the Bible not once or twice but three or more times. With each book, I strove to grasp its central message and find a way to present that message to the listening public in ten to twelve minutes—in a way that would interest them instead of making them want to tune to another station.

This book, and the two volumes that will follow, are the product of our Voice of Prophecy journey through the Bible, with many additions that have been made in the ten years since we first completed the journey series.

If you're ready to take the journey through the Book of books from cover to cover, I trust that the material we developed at the Voice of Prophecy will help you to grasp the central message of each book, and perhaps encourage you to persevere through some of the portions that may have seemed obscure or difficult to you in the past. Join me on the journey. I'm sure you won't regret it!

Ken Wade
Fall 2012

CHAPTER 1

Genesis: The Gift of Life

Genesis. It's the book of beginnings. The place where the Bible begins. The place where life on this earth begins.

You remember the story of Creation—how God created all the living things on earth, and then at last created Adam—the first man. But notice something interesting as the story is told in Genesis 2: God created all the animals and brought them to Adam so he could name them. But when that assignment was finished, Adam realized that he was lonely. There was no one like him to share the joy of life.

Genesis 2:20 describes the situation this way: "The man gave names to all the livestock, the birds of the air and all the beasts of the field. But for Adam no suitable helper was found" (NIV).

And, of course, that's where God brought someone else into the picture.

Adam was lonely, but God knew how to solve that problem. "The LORD God caused a deep sleep to fall on Adam, and he slept; and He took one of his ribs, and closed up the flesh in its place. Then the rib which the LORD God had taken from man He made into a woman, and He brought her to the man" (Genesis 2:21, 22, NKJV).

When Adam woke up, God presented him with a wonderful gift of life! A beautiful young creature, a human like him—with a few modifications, of course. Someone he could talk to and share life with on the deepest, most intimate levels.

Can you imagine what it must have been like for Adam when he first saw the woman God had created? He'd spent hours naming every creature as God paraded them in front of him: "Let's see, let's call that a cow. Let's call that one a monkey. Let's call that one a zebra."

I doubt he was giving English names to the animals, but the point is, whatever language he was speaking, he had a name for everything—until . . .

Until he saw the one creature that had been created expressly for him. I have the impression Adam was speechless, don't you? The Bible says that all he could come up with was "she shall be called 'woman,' for she was taken out of man" (verse 23, NIV). In the Hebrew language, *woman—isshah—*is simply the feminine form of the word *man.*

Swept off his feet, unable to think of anything else, Adam just called her something like *man-ess.* The feminine form of his name, *man.*

Adam and the woman were created on the sixth day of Creation week. They were the very crown of God's creation. The climax toward which all other steps of creation had been leading.

According to Genesis, man was not created as an afterthought. Everything that had been created before him was merely a prelude to the great triumphal crescendo of creation, when God would fulfill His plan to create beings in His own image and likeness to "rule over the fish of the sea and the birds of the air, over the

IN GENESIS 2, WE DISCOVER A POWERFUL KEY TO UNDERSTANDING WHY GOD CREATED ADAM AND EVE.

livestock, over all the earth, and over all the creatures that move along the ground" (Genesis 1:26, NIV).

All of life was a gift from God, and when God gave life to Adam and the woman, He placed all the rest of life in their care and keeping. They were His ambassadors and guardians, created to represent Him in caring for the rest of creation.

But there was more to God's plan than that. God didn't want just caretakers on His planet. He created creatures in His own image expressly because He wanted their friendship—He wanted to fellowship with them. In Genesis 3, we find God walking in the Garden in the cool of the evening, looking for Adam and Eve, wanting to spend time with them.

But even before that, in Genesis 2, we discover a powerful key to understanding why God created Adam and Eve.

Sometimes I've been tempted to wonder why God even bothered

creating life on this earth—considering all the heartache and trouble that it eventually led to.

But Genesis 2, verses 2 and 3, answer my question by unveiling the deeper reason behind God's action.

You see, as soon as God had finished creating the physical earth, He set aside a special time for *spiritual* development—*spiritual* creation, for developing a relationship between Himself and the ones created in His image.

EVEN IN THE TRAGIC STORY THAT UNFOLDED, SOMETHING AMAZING HAPPENED.

"By the seventh day God had finished the work he had been doing; so on the seventh day he rested from all his work. And God blessed the seventh day and made it holy, because on it he rested from all the work of creating that he had done" (Genesis 2:2, 3, NIV).

All of Creation week led up to this moment! The time when God could cease from all His activity of creating, and set aside holy Sabbath time for fellowship with the object of His creative energies: man and woman. That's why He set it aside as holy time. All the other days of the week His children would be busy tending to the tasks He had given them—caring for the world He had created. But on this day, He would rest—physically; and they would rest—physically. But His work of creation would continue on a *spiritual* level, as the ones created in God's image became friends with their God, and He infused more and more of His Spirit into them, and they grew to be more and more like Him—more and more in His image.

That was God's plan.

Unfortunately, things didn't all go according to plan.

But even in the tragic story that unfolded, something amazing happened.

You know the story. The woman was tempted by the serpent; she tempted Adam; and both of them ended up sinning and losing their right to live eternally in the Garden of Eden.

But do you know what's really amazing here? It's only after this great tragedy that the woman received a name. It was only then that Adam got around to giving her a name. And the name he chose makes the story even more astonishing.

Now, if you were Adam, what would you call someone who had

been instrumental in leading you into a crime that earned you the death penalty?

Maybe you can think of some names you'd want to call a person like that—probably none of them complimentary.

But notice this in Genesis 3:20, as it is worded in the New English Bible: "The man called his wife Eve because she was the mother of all who live." And a footnote in the New English Bible gives a translation of the name *Eve*.

Here's what it says: "*That is* Life."

Did you catch that? After the great tragedy of sin that led to death, Adam looked at his wife and gave her a name: Life!

What a marvelous story! What a fantastic testimony to the understanding of our first father!

Some people say that the first stories in Genesis demean the role of the woman and make her into a scapegoat. But Adam certainly didn't do that.

> AFTER THE GREAT TRAGEDY OF SIN THAT LED TO DEATH, ADAM LOOKED AT HIS WIFE AND GAVE HER A NAME: LIFE!

Even after she had played a significant role in bringing death to our planet, Adam looked at his dear wife—the beloved gift he had received from God—and he named her Life! She was indeed the gift of life, for without her, human life—Adam's life—could not continue through descendants. Human history would have been very short in the absence of this gift of life.

The story of Adam and Eve is just one of the many great stories in the book of Genesis. As you read on through the book, you'll discover that story after story focuses on God's gift of life to humanity.

Sure there's the terrible story of the Flood, where so much life was lost. But even in that story, we find that God made provisions for life to go on. He warned Noah about what was coming and told him to build an ark and to "bring into the ark two of all living creatures, male and female, *to keep them alive with you*" (Genesis 6:19, NIV; emphasis added).

God made it plain that He was not in the business of destroying life, but of preserving life. At the end of the Flood story, God made a covenant—a contract—with all living things, promising that He would never again destroy all life on the earth.

So even this tragic story reveals how God gave life, and what He did to preserve life on our planet.

And as we move on through the book of Genesis, we come to one of the most compelling stories in all of world literature: the story of Abraham. Here is a man who answered God's call to move out in faith, trusting simply that God would show him where to go, and would preserve his life when he got there. Abraham also had to trust God to fulfill His promise of a son to preserve the life of his family line.

Here is the story of a man who actually met and talked with God face-to-face, and pled with God for the lives of the people living in Sodom and Gomorrah (see Genesis 18). It is the story of a God who is merciful and so insistent on saving lives, that His angels pulled Abraham's nephew Lot and his family almost kicking and screaming out of Sodom to spare them from destruction.

The promise of life

But the most powerful story about the preservation of life is the one found in Genesis 22: the account of Abraham's journey, accompanied by his son Isaac, to the top of Mount Moriah. Father and son climb that steep hill, the son carrying the wood to offer a burnt offering to the God his father has taught him to love and trust, the God who has worked a miracle of life so that this boy could be born, even though his mother was far past childbearing age.

> HIS WORDS SPRING FROM A DEEP WELL OF UNDERSTANDING OF THE GOD HE WORSHIPS.

And as they near the top of the hill, Isaac looks around, thinking that his dear old father has forgotten one important detail: "Father," he says, "Here are the fire and the wood, but where is the young beast for the sacrifice?" (Genesis 22:7, NEB).

Abraham has come to this place bearing a heart-rending secret. God has called him to bring his son to the mountain to slay *him* as a sacrifice.

How can he answer his son's question?

I imagine there was a long pause.

Then I see Abraham sitting down on one of the stones they had been dragging into place to create an altar, resting his head on his hands.

When he finally speaks, his words spring from a deep well of understanding of the God he worships. But I think I hear a tremor, a wave of prescient grief in his voice as he speaks. "God will provide himself with a young beast for a sacrifice, my son," he says (verse 8, NEB).

Abraham has learned through long experience to have faith in God's promises. Isaac, his son, is God's gift—the answer to a century of prayers. No doubt it is a struggle for Abraham to understand how God's plan can include taking away this gift of life as a sacrifice. But he answers in confidence, saying, "God will provide."

Go back and read the story again in Genesis 22. Relish the tension, every emotion that surges through the interaction between Abraham and his God, and between Abraham and his son.

It's a powerful story that ends with the gift of life—and a promise.

God provides a substitute—a ram that can be sacrificed in place of Isaac, sparing the boy's life. And in that powerful story is a marvelous promise from our God, the God who wants to give each of us the gift of life. It is the powerful promise of a Savior who would one day sacrifice His life on a mountain near Moriah in order to give *life* to all who would accept the gift.

> RELISH THE TENSION, EVERY EMOTION THAT SURGES THROUGH THE INTERACTION BETWEEN ABRAHAM AND HIS GOD.

"God so loved the world, that he gave his only begotten Son, that whosoever believeth in him should not perish, but have everlasting life" (John 3:16).

There are more stories in Genesis. The story of Isaac and his descendants, and of Jacob and his journey back to Mesopotamia, where God blesses him with abundant flocks—the gift of life overflowing to him in miraculous ways despite the conniving of his uncle Laban.

Genesis ends with the story of Jacob's son Joseph and his miraculous recovery from what seems like a death sentence. When his brothers sell him into slavery, it seems that his life has been sacrificed. But things turn out very differently from what the brothers had planned. In Egypt, God uses Joseph to spare life—by God's grace the gift of life was preserved in thousands of people during a terrible famine.

Genesis. It's the story of the Gift of Life. The story of God's grace bursting forth in life for humanity, over and over again!

CHAPTER 2

Exodus: Free to Follow

Comfortable.

That's how the people would remember their lives in Egypt—even though they and their ancestors had been enslaved there for centuries, even though their suffering had led them to cry out to the Lord for deliverance.

It's amazing, isn't it, how quickly our memories of the past fade when we run up against obstacles in what were supposed to be our "new and improved" lives. Suddenly, when the going got tough, the Israelites who had left Egypt to follow Moses to the Promised Land were struck with serious cases of amnesia.

Oh, sure, they could still remember the taskmasters who had made their lives miserable by demanding that they make more and more bricks with less and less raw materials. And there was, of course, the problem of all the boy babies being thrown into the river!

But no place is perfect, after all. With memories fading of how they had suffered and how they had cried out for deliverance, they decided that slavery actually hadn't been such a bad profession all in all.

Sitting around campfires out in the desert, scratching fleas and grinding sand between their teeth after dinner, they began to think that life would have been better if only Moses hadn't come along and upset their miserable, peaceful existence by demanding that they be "set free." After all, wasn't it really his fault that the taskmasters had taken to treating them so badly? It was his demands that had angered Pharaoh and led to their increased misery.

Thinking back on it now, they could come up with all kinds of things for which to blame Moses.

Exodus is a book about liberation—about God freeing His people from bondage. But whenever you talk about freedom, you also need to think about the responsibilities that freedom brings with it.

It wasn't long before the people whom God had liberated discovered that freedom brings heavy responsibilities. And it made them stop and ask, Just how important is this freedom, anyhow?

In the New Testament, the deliverance of the Israelites from Egypt is used as an example of how God wants to free us from our bondage to sin.

And what happened with the Israelites sometimes happens to us, too, doesn't it? Once we've been freed from negative habits, after a while the old habits start looking attractive again—even though we know they were destroying our lives, even though we pled with God to deliver us. And we start "longing for the fleshpots of Egypt."

We can take away many lessons from reading the book of Exodus. The most important, perhaps, being that God wants to free us from bondage—even though He knows that once we're free, we may blame Him for the difficulties we encounter while exercising the freedom He has given us!

You probably remember the story of how God went about freeing His people from bondage—bringing plagues of increasing severity upon the Egyptians until Pharaoh was forced to acknowledge the superior power of the God of the Hebrews.

And when the day of deliverance finally came, the people went streaming out of their slave encampment into the desert by the light of a full moon on the fifteenth day of the month of Abib.

Behind them the wails of Egyptians whose first-born sons had died in the tenth plague filled the cities with commotion and despair. But there was no despair among the Israelites. They had only a bright future of freedom to look forward to.

> HE KNOWS THAT ONCE WE'RE FREE, WE MAY BLAME HIM FOR THE DIFFICULTIES WE ENCOUNTER WHILE EXERCISING THE FREEDOM HE HAS GIVEN US!

It wasn't long, though, before they began to think the burden of freedom was too heavy. As part of God's plan to let them see His power, and to teach them to trust in Him, He deliberately led them in a way that made the Egyptians think they were confused and lost in the desert—you can read about that in Exodus 14:1–4.

But when Pharaoh took the bait and came out in hot pursuit, the joy of freedom suddenly turned to the insecurity of fear for their very lives! The Israelites no longer had the security of their humdrum slave lives. They needed to learn to walk by faith in God, not by faith in Pharaoh. And they weren't quite ready to do that.

As Pharaoh drew near, the Israelites looked back, and there were the Egyptians advancing on them. In great fear the Israelites cried out to the Lord. They said to Moses, "Was it because there were no graves in Egypt that you have taken us away to die in the wilderness? What have you done to us, bringing us out of Egypt? Is this not the very thing we told you in Egypt, 'Let us alone and let us serve the Egyptians'? For it would have been better for us to serve the Egyptians than to die in the wilderness" (Exodus 14:10–12, NRSV).

That happened by the Red Sea, and we all know the story of how God delivered them by opening a way for them through the sea. Which led to Miriam's great, jubilant song:

And Miriam sang to them:
"Sing to the LORD, for he has triumphed gloriously;
horse and rider he has thrown into the sea" (Exodus 15:21, NRSV).

These ups and downs all happened within the first month after Moses led the people out of Egypt. Exodus 16 tells what happened at the very next full moon—a month to the day after they had been liberated.

I can picture some of the people sitting around the campfire, out under the stars, worrying out loud about their future. As the night begins to turn chilly, they start reminiscing about what it had been like back in Egypt. And before long the reminiscing turns to what we today call dissing. They diss on Moses, they diss on Aaron, and for that matter, if you cared for their opinion, they'd tell you that they didn't really care for God Himself, or the path He was leading them along. Notice this complaining in Exodus 16:1–3: "On the fifteenth day of the second month [They had left Egypt on the fifteenth day of the first month. See Exodus 12:1, 2ff.] after they had departed from the land of Egypt the whole congregation of the Israelites complained against Moses and Aaron in the wilderness. The Israelites said to them, 'If only we had died by the hand of the LORD in the land of Egypt, when we sat by the fleshpots and ate our fill of bread; for you have brought us out into this wilderness to kill this whole assembly with hunger' " (NRSV).

How quickly they forgot the misery they had endured as Pharaoh's slaves! No one seemed to remember that the reason Moses had come to deliver them from slavery was that God had heard their miserable groaning.

> REALLY THEY'RE LIKE SO MANY OF US: COMFORTABLE IN OUR MISERY AND RELISHING THE RIGHT TO CARP ABOUT IT!

In fact, the reason they found themselves out in the wilderness, following Moses, was simple. It's found in Exodus 2:23: the Israelites groaned in their slavery and cried out, and their cry for help was heard in heaven.

God tuned in to their cries and asked Moses to go to the rescue. And that is how they ended up out in the desert, sitting around a campfire, complaining about their fate.

And this belly-aching episode was by no means unique in their experience. In fact, it's just page one in a litany of poor-me episodes. It happens over and over again throughout the book of Exodus.

The people complain.

God responds to their complaints and presents a solution.

Then the people complain about the solution.

But these people are not some malicious mob of maligning malcontents. You realize that they're a pretty normal group when you stop to think about it. The stories in Exodus are about real people going at life in a very human way. Which of us hasn't done the same sort of thing—complained and complained until things finally changed—and then we complained about the changes!

Exodus is a book that reveals a lot about human nature. My human nature—and perhaps yours too. It's a book about people who think they want a change, but really they're like so many of us: comfortable in our misery and relishing the right to carp about it!

It's not easy to get people to move out of their comfort zones.

It's not easy to get *me* to move out of my comfort zone. And even when I do, if things start going wrong, I'm likely to start wondering whether I shouldn't have just stayed back where everything was easier.

But God had a plan for Israel, and He has a plan for your life and mine. That plan often involves responding to His call for us to try something new and different.

For Israel it meant a journey out into the wilderness—out to an austere mountain called Sinai, where they had an encounter with the Divine that they would never forget:

> There was thunder and lightning as well as a thick cloud on the mountain, and a blast of a trumpet so loud that all the people who were in the camp trembled. Moses brought the people out of the camp to meet God. They took their stand at the foot of the mountain. Now Mount Sinai was wrapped in smoke, because the LORD had descended upon it in fire; the smoke went up like the smoke of a kiln, while the whole mountain shook violently. As the blast of the trumpet grew louder and louder, Moses would speak and God would answer him in thunder (Exodus 19:16–19, NRSV).

This awesome demonstration of power left no doubt in anyone's mind that they had come to the right place to find God.

The only question left was, Did they really *want* to find Him? Did they *want* to live in His community? Or would they prefer to have the Egyptians for neighbors?

> THEY HAD COME TO THE RIGHT PLACE TO FIND GOD. THE ONLY QUESTION LEFT WAS, DID THEY REALLY *WANT* TO FIND HIM?

When the opportunity to be neighbors with God presented itself, the people suddenly backed away. "When the people saw the thunder and lightning and heard the trumpet and saw the mountain in smoke, they trembled with fear. They stayed at a distance and said to Moses, 'Speak to us yourself and we will listen. But do not have God speak to us or we will die' " (Exodus 20:18, 19, NIV).

They were frightened. Who wouldn't have been?

They didn't really want to hear the voice of God.

And that raises another question.

There was a time when I was sure I wanted to hear the voice of

God speaking directly to me—answering all my questions.

But the longer I've lived, the more I've come to wonder: Do I *really* want to hear the voice of God? Do I really want Him to tell me what to do and what not to do?

How about you?

How would you have responded to the voice of God, if you had been there at the foot of the mountain?

To the Israelites' credit, "They responded, 'We will do everything the Lord has said; we will obey' " (Exodus 24:7, NIV).

Well, how else could they have responded under the circumstances?

It was a natural human response to the fireworks display they had just seen. But a few weeks later, after things had calmed down on the mountaintop, their reaction was a bit different. Suddenly they were seized with another longing for "back home in Egypt." They even went so far as to make themselves a god like the bull gods worshiped beside the Nile.

The story of how Moses' brother, Aaron, molded a golden calf for the people to worship while Moses was

> Exodus challenges us to accept the freedom God gives us.

up on Mount Sinai is told in Exodus 32. It's a tragic story of mistrust, faltering faith, and failed fidelity.

But even that rebellion became a learning experience for the people who had chosen to follow God out into the wilderness. After God told Moses that He was ready to abandon the people who had abandoned Him, Moses pled with God to take his life instead of destroying all the people. And that experience taught a powerful lesson.

It was a powerful illustration to the people of just how much Moses cared about them. And beyond that, they also learned that the God they had met at Sinai was not just a thunder- and lightning-storm deity. He also had a gracious, forgiving, loving nature that clearly wanted the best for them.

The thunder and lightning and trumpets were no doubt a necessary display to get the attention of people who up to that time had responded only to the authority of the whip—and weren't ready to respond to a simple invitation to obey the Lord.

The lightning and thunder would be an important part of their relationship with Him. But so would the grace of a forgiving Father.

The forty chapters of Exodus, of course, contain much more. A lot of description; pages of instructions on how to build a tabernacle where God would dwell in the center of the nation; lengthy descriptions of how priests should dress and what they should do.

These are all important elements in God's plan to communicate both His love and His justice, His mercy and His righteousness to His people.

But the book of Exodus is well summed up in the brief vignettes I've mentioned: God delivering His people from slavery; God's giving of the law; the people's natural responses; and the people's all-too-normal longing to go back to simpler times when they didn't have to respond to a God who was personally interested in them.

The lesson of the book is clear: God loves His children; He wants us to be with Him; He will be faithful and true to us.

And the challenge is clear as well. Exodus challenges us to accept the freedom God gives us, but also to respond to His leading and to trust that the path He is taking us down leads to the Promised Land.

Even when it's bumpy.

I want to take that challenge and let God lead me to the eternal Promised Land. How about you?

CHAPTER 3

Leviticus: He Lived With Us

The people of Israel had followed their God out into the wilderness.

Well, really, they had followed Moses—hoping he would take them to meet God.

Day after day they traveled through barren countryside on foot, struggling up sandy hills and down into valleys where the heat was so oppressive, the air so thick, that just breathing was a chore. Marching on toward Canaan must have seemed to them at times an impossible task in quest of an impossible dream.

GOD'S SCHEDULE DOESN'T ALWAYS MESH WITH OUR IMPATIENCE FOR INSTANT RESULTS.

Moses had answered God's call to go to Egypt and lead His people out of slavery into the wilderness to meet with their God. But when the Israelites finally were able to leave Egypt, they soon learned that life on the road isn't always easy. Beset by heat, hunger, sand, dust, and overpowering thirst, they can hardly be blamed for beginning to wonder if they were simply fools being led in search of gold at the end of an elusive rainbow.

Do you ever find yourself feeling that way? As if you've answered God's call—stepped out in faith—and set out to follow His leading, but all it gets you are trials and hard marches that seem to lead nowhere?

Don't be discouraged. You're actually in good company with Moses and the people God called him to lead.

The problem—from our perspective, anyway—is that God's schedule doesn't always mesh with our impatience for instant results.

It takes faith to learn to trust His plan. Our part is to be sure we are following His leading: Continuing to listen for His voice, as it is revealed in His Written Word, the Bible. Walking in His plan and being patient.

As the book of Leviticus reveals, God often has something in mind for us that is far better than what we could plan for ourselves. And often our preparation for being part of His plan involves learning lessons through the experiences He gives us along the way.

That was the case with the people of Israel on the way to Mount Sinai.

When we looked at the book of Exodus, we witnessed the people's reaction when they finally met God.

It was an encounter with the Divine that they would never forget: "There was thunder and lightning, as well as a thick cloud on the mountain, and a blast of a trumpet so loud that all the people who were in the camp trembled. . . . Now Mount Sinai was wrapped in smoke, because the LORD had descended upon it in fire; the smoke went up like the smoke of a kiln, while the whole mountain shook violently" (Exodus 19:16–18, NRSV).

> THEY WERE QUICK TO WORK OUT A DEAL WITH MOSES.

This awesome demonstration of power left no doubt in anyone's mind that they had come to the right place to find God. The only question left was, Did they really *want* to find Him? Did they *want* to live with Him? Or would they be better off back serving the Egyptians instead?

"When the people saw the thunder and lightning and heard the trumpet and saw the mountain in smoke, they trembled with fear. They stayed at a distance and said to Moses, 'Speak to us yourself and we will listen. But do not have God speak to us or we will die' " (Exodus 20:18, 19, NIV).

They were quick to work out a deal with Moses, telling him, "You go up on the mountain and talk to God; then come back down and tell us what He said. We aren't worthy to be in God's presence, and besides that, He scares us!"

So Moses went up on Mount Sinai, and we all know the story of how he brought the Ten Commandments down with him.

But that's not all he brought down with him. He brought something else as well—something with which you might be less familiar. He brought instructions for building a "tabernacle" in which God could live among His people.

> THE TABERNACLE DEMONSTRATED THE IMMENSE VALUE GOD PLACED UPON MAINTAINING A CLOSE RELATIONSHIP WITH HIS PEOPLE.

They spent the next year camped beside the mountain, building this tabernacle—which was kind of a portable temple, constructed mainly of fine fabrics and animal skins, with a good bit of gold thrown in to add luster and demonstrate the immense value God placed upon maintaining a close relationship with His people.

The book of Exodus records the instructions for building the tabernacle. The book of Leviticus is filled with instructions for the priests who would minister the grace of God in that tabernacle.

If you take the time to read through the book of Leviticus, as I hope you will, notice how detailed the instructions are.

Now, I have to admit, Leviticus is not easy reading. Especially if you don't understand the symbolism behind all of the things that are being described. It's easy to get bogged down when reading about various types of offerings, and what a priest is supposed to wear, and how to deal with a case of leprosy in a primitive desert camp.

But trust me: you can gain some amazing insights into God's plan of salvation by studying these seemingly mysterious ceremonies and instructions. Many useful books and commentaries that can help you understand the text are available. I recently checked the Internet and found that copies of a book by Dr. Leslie Hardinge, who first inspired my interest in the tabernacle during a series of meetings he presented while I was in college, is still available. His book *Shadows of His Sacrifice: Studies in the Sanctuary* is available through Amazon.com

> YOU CAN GAIN SOME AMAZING INSIGHTS INTO GOD'S PLAN OF SALVATION BY STUDYING THESE SEEMINGLY MYSTERIOUS CEREMONIES.

and other booksellers. It's just a short book, but it gives amazing insights into the significance of many of the interesting details about the sanctuary that you find when you are reading Leviticus.

God's plan for saving human beings by His grace is revealed more clearly in this tabernacle than almost any other place in the Old Testament. But it takes careful, dedicated study to see the depth and beauty of the plan.

This tabernacle worship-center had an outer courtyard surrounded by a high, curtained fence. Inside that courtyard was a tent made primarily of animal skins.

That tent was to be the center of Israel's worship and knowledge of God. That was where God Himself would live!

The people who had journeyed across the desert with Moses, and who had witnessed the clouds and smoke and fire on top of Mount Sinai, already knew that their God was a Holy God whom they could not approach directly.

> GOD IS, AFTER ALL, TOO BIG TO BE CAPTURED WITH PAINT OR IN STONE OR CLAY OR BRONZE IMAGES.

They had received His commandments that forbade them from making statues or pictures to represent Him. God is, after all, too big to be captured with paint or in stone or clay or bronze images.

And the people no doubt still felt a measure of fright when they thought of approaching God. After the display of power they had seen, it would be only natural for them to want to keep their distance from Him.

But God wanted them close. When He had them build the tabernacle, where do you suppose He had them put it?

Right in the middle of their campground!

Right at the center of their lives! Not off on the edge. Not up on some Mount Olympus, far away and aloof.

Right at the core of their community.

That's where God always wants to be—for us as well—in the center of our lives, not off on the fringes!

Right there in the center of Israel's campground, God set up a kind of schoolroom to teach His people about Himself.

So, what was it that He wanted to teach them?

That He is a God who gives life, a God of grace, and a God of purity.

Admittedly, it may not seem that way to you when you first read the book of Leviticus. The first seventeen chapters are all about killing animals as sacrifices. So how can I say that God revealed Himself as a God of life and grace?

Well, remember this: in agricultural and hunting societies, people regard the death of an animal far differently from the way we see it in our industrial society. I've read, for instance, that when Native Americans would kill a buffalo, they would hold a ceremony to thank the spirit of the buffalo for coming to them to give them life. The death of the animal was recognized, not as a slaughter, but as the animal's gracious gift of its life to the people.

LEVITICUS HELPS YOU UNDERSTAND SACRIFICE DIFFERENTLY FROM HOW WE MIGHT VIEW IT.

When you read Leviticus with that mind-set, it helps you understand sacrifice differently from how we might view it from our modern perspective. We tend to think in one direction only—we think of a man who has committed a sin, who realizes that he must now sacrifice one of his animals to atone for his sin.

But what if we take it from the opposite perspective?

What if we see, instead, a man who is planning to butcher a lamb for his family to eat. The laws of Leviticus simply tell him where and how to kill it.

Many people who read Leviticus miss this fact: the majority of the sacrifices described there do not involve burning the entire animal on the altar. Usually it was only the fat portions that were to be burned. The rest of the meat was divided between the priest and the person bringing the sacrifice.

The basic rule regarding sacrifice is found in Leviticus 17:3, 4: "Whatever man of the house of Israel who kills an ox or lamb or goat in the camp, or who kills it outside the camp, and does not bring it to the door of the tabernacle of meeting to offer an offering to the LORD before the tabernacle of the LORD, the guilt of bloodshed shall be imputed to that man. He has shed blood; and that man shall be cut off from among his people" (NKJV).

The idea is clear: when you're going to butcher an animal, bring it as an offering—remember that its meat not only provides you physical food, but spiritual nourishment as well—it brings you peace with God as you confess your sin and accept the death of the animal in your place.

This puts an entirely different perspective on the book of Leviticus. If you're a vegetarian or a person who buys your ground chuck and sirloin steak at the supermarket, you never have to give much thought to where the meat comes from. In fact, you may prefer *not* to think about it.

But in a society of shepherds, taking the life of an animal was a fairly commonplace event.

Rather than instructing people to kill animals, the book of Leviticus instructs people on how, where, and when to do it.

It instructs God's people: Don't make it a commonplace event that you do just anywhere. When it comes time for an animal to die, take its life respectfully. Consider

USE THE MOMENT OF THE ANIMAL'S DEATH AS A TIME TO COMMEMORATE GOD'S GRACE IN FORGIVING YOUR SINS.

that God is the Giver of all life, and that in taking a life, you are demonstrating the results of sin. Use the moment of the animal's death as a time to commemorate God's grace in forgiving your sins.

While the people may not have understood this in detail, the sacrifice of an animal pointed forward to the death of Jesus on the cross in our place.

When the animal gave up its life in order to provide life to humans, the experience should have reminded people of how God used animal skins to keep Adam and Eve warm when the chill of sin first descended upon them. And it should have helped them look forward to the Redeemer who would die in their place as well.

There's another fascinating fact about these sacrifices that seems to demonstrate God's concern for His people as well. When you read Leviticus, notice that God always had the priests burn the fat of the offering on the altar. The people were not to eat either the fat or the blood.

Could it be that here we see God being concerned for His people's cardiac health? "If you must eat meat, eat only lean meat" is a mantra we hear all the time from health professionals today!

When you really understand Leviticus, you see that it, along with the rest of the Bible, reveals a God of grace. A God who wants to forgive His people. A God who wants to be with His people—right in the center of their lives. A God who makes it possible for them to come to Him without fear!

Leviticus 16 in particular makes a fascinating study, as you consider the activities of the most important day of the Hebrew calendar—the Day of Atonement. In a series of sacrifices and ceremonies, the priests demonstrated to the people that the sins of the entire nation were being forgiven by the grace of God, who would bear the responsibility Himself. Every time the high priest sprinkled blood on the ark of the covenant in the Most Holy Place, it pointed forward to the time when Jesus would bear the weight of all the world's sins on Calvary.

> IT POINTED FORWARD TO THE TIME WHEN JESUS WOULD BEAR THE WEIGHT OF ALL THE WORLD'S SINS ON CALVARY.

This day of grace was to be right at the center of God's people's lives. It came right in the middle of their annual calendar. Just at the time when they expected the early rains to bring new life to their land. God's grace and the gift of new life were to be linked together in their minds, and right at the center of their hearts. Just as the tabernacle was to be right at the center of their camp.

How is it with you today? Is God at the center of your life? He wants to be there. He wants to have a tabernacle, right in your heart, where you worship Him, and where you come seeking His grace and forgiveness for your sins.

He lived with the people of Israel in their camp. He invited them to come to Him in worship, to be cleansed of their sins, and to be close to Him, appreciating both His holiness and His grace. And He invites us to do the same.

CHAPTER 4

Numbers: Marching to Zion

What does it mean to be a person of faith? To really trust in the Lord?

Is it just a matter of saying "I believe," or is there more to it than that?

Such questions faced the Israelites who had followed Moses out of Egypt when it came time for them to go in and possess the land that God had promised to them.

The story is told in the biblical book we know as Numbers, but it is known in the Hebrew Bible as "In the Wilderness." Much of the book focuses on the Israelites' journey from the time they left Mount Sinai until they finally were ready to enter the Promised Land nearly forty years later.

Their faith was frequently tested during this time. And they seemed to spend a lot of their time grousing about their leadership and their God. In phraseology that almost became a mantra, we find them saying over and over again, "I wish we had never left Egypt. We had plenty to eat there. We ought to go back!"

But in one of the stories told in Numbers, they take it a step further and even hold an election to choose leaders who will take them back to Egypt!

What's going on here? We may wonder, Don't these people have even a smidgen of faith in God's leading?

It's easy to find ourselves shaking our heads and wondering what was the matter with the Israelites when we're sitting in easy chairs, reading about their adventures.

But it's one thing to read about someone else's struggles, and quite another when the struggles are our own, isn't it? How many times have *I* failed to move forward in faith, simply because I thought the risks were too great?

When we're talking about throwing ourselves into battle—into hand-to-hand combat with people who are defending their very own ancestral lands, the risk level is pretty high!

When you think about it that way, it's a bit easier to empathize with the men who came back after spying out the land of Canaan and brought a negative report.

You remember the story, don't you, how Moses sent twelve men—leaders of the twelve tribes—into Canaan to explore it in preparation for an invasion. And of those twelve men, only two brought back positive reports.

The majority report went like this: "The land we explored devours those living in it. All the people we saw there are of great size. We saw the Nephilim. . . . We seemed like grasshoppers in our own eyes, and we looked the same to them" (Numbers 13:32, 33, NIV).

Ten of twelve spies brought back that report to Moses after they had explored the land that God had promised to give them. They had gone out full of optimism, excited to be exploring the place to which they were planning to move. They returned full of pessimism, afraid to even think about claiming God's promises.

Winston Churchill said, "A pessimist sees the difficulty in every opportunity; an optimist sees the opportunity in every difficulty."

Unfortunately, ten out of twelve of the men Moses sent to check out the Promised Land were thoroughgoing pessimists.

> CALEB AND JOSHUA TURNED THE WORDS BACK ON THEIR FAITHLESS COMPATRIOTS.

The group contained only two optimists: Caleb and Joshua. They went to all the same places; they saw all the same things. They probably felt just as "grasshopperish" beside the sons of Anak as the rest of the men did.

But how did they respond to the challenge?

Here's what they said: "The land we passed through and explored is exceedingly good. If the LORD is pleased with us, he will lead us into that land, a land flowing with milk and honey, and will give it to us.

Only do not rebel against the LORD. And *do not be afraid* of the people of the land, because *we will swallow them up.* Their protection is gone, but the LORD is with us. Do not be afraid of them" (Numbers 14:7–9, NIV; emphasis added).

Notice the strong contrast here. The first group delivered the majority report: "The land we explored *devours* the people."

In their minority report, Caleb and Joshua turned the words back on their faithless compatriots: "Don't be afraid of those people. *We will swallow them up!*"

> WHY DID THE LORD HAVE
> MOSES BOTHER WITH
> SENDING SPIES INTO THE
> LAND IN THE FIRST PLACE?

The majority report would be almost laughable if it weren't for the pain and problems it caused. Notice that the ten spies reported that a lot of really big and scary people lived in the land, but in the same breath they said that the land devoured its inhabitants!

What were they really afraid of? The land, or the people? Or were they simply afraid to go forward, clinging to the promises of God?

When you read the story of the spies in Numbers 13, you might notice something that seems a little bit odd about how this whole situation came about. Here's how the story begins: "The LORD said to Moses, 'Send men to spy out the land of Canaan, which I am giving to the Israelites.' . . .

"Moses sent them to spy out the land of Canaan, and said to them, 'Go up . . . and see what the land is like, and whether the people who live in it are strong or weak, whether they are few or many, and whether the land they live in is good or bad, and whether the towns that they live in are unwalled or fortified, and whether the land is rich or poor, and whether there are trees in it or not' " (Numbers 13:1, 2, 17–20, NRSV).

The thing I find myself wondering about in the story is, Why did the Lord have Moses bother with sending spies into the land in the first place?

In other words, if God is leading in your life, why take the time to scout out the territory ahead? Why not just march in double time, and let God worry about the terrain, how big the people are, and whether there are trees or walls or anything else there?

Sometimes God does expect us to just step out in faith, without

37

telling us much about where we're going. He did that with Abraham when He called him to go to the land of Canaan. But in this instance, with a large group of people, He chose a different method. He told them to send spies and to find out as much about the land as possible before they entered it.

Do you think that perhaps this was part of God's training program for His people? That He wanted them to know exactly what lay ahead and to learn to move forward in faith, even when fear gripped their hearts? That they were to learn to exercise faith against their fears on the way into battle—not just expect to develop faith when they were face-to-face with their enemies?

> ALL THEY COULD THINK ABOUT WAS THEIR FEARS, NOT THEIR FAITH.

Unfortunately, the people didn't respond with faith. It seemed that as soon as they heard the majority report, they forgot all the miracles and faith-building experiences God had already led them through. All they could think about was their fears, not their faith.

And fear and faith don't mix well. One or the other has to rule. Every day we choose our master. Will it be faith, or will it be fear? Will we stand with the minority report, or will we fall with the majority? Am I a Joshua, or am I a Shammua?

Shammua was one of the spies who could see only obstacles and problems where Joshua and Caleb saw opportunities and promises. Shammua couldn't take his stand with the optimists who said, "The land is good, and God is good. If He wants to give us the land, then the land won't devour us. The people won't defeat us. We will do the devouring!"

> THE BOOK OF NUMBERS BOTHERS A LOT OF PEOPLE.

Now, before we go on to tell the rest of the story, I want to pause for us to wrestle with some of the difficulties this story brings to our minds as we read through the Bible.

The book of Numbers bothers a lot of people. The central story in the book concerns the Israelites' belief that God had given them a land—and that they were to take that land from the people who had lived there and considered it their ancestral land for generations.

If a group of people were to try doing that sort of thing today, we'd probably accuse them of ethnic cleansing. It's just not politically correct for one group of people to declare that God has told them to take over another group's houses, vineyards, and olive orchards. In fact, the conflict over ancestral ownership continues to play out in ancient Canaan even to this day.

Recently, I had the opportunity to visit the nation known today as the Hashemite Kingdom of Jordan. It's the country on the east side of the Jordan River—the very land from which the Israelites eventually attacked Canaan under Joshua's leadership.

I learned that many Palestinian refugees who were driven out of their ancestral homeland more than forty years ago in the Six-Day War, still wear their house keys on neck chains—the keys to the houses that their families owned for generations, but were driven out of in 1967 by the descendants of the people who followed Moses out of Egypt.

> WHEN YOU READ THROUGH THE BIBLE THOUGHTFULLY, YOU WILL NO DOUBT COME UPON PARTS THAT DISTURB YOU.

As other nations in the region develop weapons of mass destruction, the question of whose god has deeded his people what land continues to grab the headlines today and keeps the armies of superpowers stoked and at the ready to defend one side or another.

And at the root of this modern conflict, if you trace it back, lies varying interpretations of stories found in the Bible, especially those found in Numbers.

When you read through the Bible thoughtfully, particularly the Old Testament, you will no doubt come upon parts that disturb you—certain stories that just don't mesh with the way people think today. Stories that don't seem to be "politically correct" to us.

People today naturally ask questions, such as, How could Moses be *so sure* that God was telling him to drive the Canaanites out of their country, killing and pillaging all through the land?

How could the same God who issued the commandment "Thou shalt not kill" then proceed to tell His people to go into the land and wipe out the inhabitants, leaving only the unmarried women as survivors—and even taking them captive, to mingle their seed with the offspring of His chosen nation?

It's difficult for us to understand, but if we're going to take the Bible seriously, and if we're going to read it faithfully, we will come up against such questions. And it seems to me that the best answer we can give is that God was dealing with a less-than-an-ideal situation.

The book of Numbers, let's face it, is one of the "messy" parts of the Bible. I like to think of the Bible as a sandwich. In the first book, Genesis, everything begins perfectly. And in the last book, Revelation, everything is restored to perfection. But the parts in the middle of the sandwich often get a bit messy. What comes between the ideal world of Genesis and the ideal world of Revelation is far from perfect.

> THE BOOK OF NUMBERS, LET'S FACE IT, IS ONE OF THE "MESSY" PARTS OF THE BIBLE.

Because of sin, God has to deal with rebellious people in all their frailties and foibles. He has to work with the customs, the understanding, and the abilities of the people He's dealing with.

Remember as you read Numbers that He had just recently delivered the Israelites from slavery in a land with thousands of other gods. He had seen that His people were easily sidetracked into worshiping other gods. Now He wanted to settle them in a new land and teach them to worship Him faithfully. He couldn't allow them to begin worshiping other gods again.

So God originally planned to drive out the current inhabitants, who worshiped a pantheon of gods, in a more gentle way.

"I will send the hornet ahead of you to drive the Hivites, Canaanites and Hittites out of your way," He promised in Exodus 23:28 (NIV).

He wanted to gently and slowly open up the land to give His people a place to live. (Incidentally—going back to the story of Abraham— archaeologists tell us that at the time God first promised the land to him, Canaan was sparsely populated. Weather conditions and other factors had caused its earlier inhabitants to die out naturally or to move to more fertile, better-irrigated lands. So this type of gradually opening up the land had happened before.)

But, in the case of the Israelites under Moses' leadership, things didn't work out according to God's ideal plan.

When Shammua and his friends brought back a negative, fearful report from their spying mission, the people rebelled against God and refused to go into the land. They even went so far as to plan an election to choose a leader to take them back to Egypt! They were ready to kill Moses and Aaron and take over their own destinies. They wanted to follow someone who would listen to *them* instead of to God.

Now, democracy is a great idea. It serves many nations well. But these people had the opportunity to have something far better: direct guidance by God through His prophet Moses. And they didn't want it.

It's a tragic story—but, oh how *human* a story. How natural, how normal for human beings to want to be masters of their own destinies. How natural for me—for you—to want things our own way instead of God's way.

For the people of Israel, their rebellion turned into a horrible tragedy. God told them they could have their way—they could stay out in the wilderness instead of going into the Promised Land.

But then, acting like spoiled children who always have to have their own way, when their Parent gave in and said, "Fine, have it your way," they suddenly wanted the opposite!

So Israel rebelled again and marched off to try to take the land on their own. It was a horrible mistake that led to ignominious defeat and great loss of life. Finally, all of them died outside the Promised Land during forty years of wilderness wandering. All of them, that is, except for two: Caleb and Joshua, the men with faith.

> DEMOCRACY IS A GREAT IDEA. BUT THESE PEOPLE HAD THE OPPORTUNITY TO HAVE SOMETHING FAR BETTER.

You know, all of us are making a journey—a journey to the Land of Promise, heaven, "sweet Canaan's happy land." God's Word is filled with instructions and promises to help us along the way. But on whose side do we find it easier to come down—the optimist's or the pessimist's? Don't you want to be like Caleb, like Joshua, a man or woman of faith who claims the promises and walks with God all the way to the Promised Land?

CHAPTER 5

Deuteronomy: Divine Reminders

As we read the book of Numbers, we found ourselves dealing with some difficult questions about God's sense of justice and what happens when human rights seem to run counter to divine mandates.

As you read through Deuteronomy, you may once again find yourself puzzling over things you read—divine mandates that rub us the wrong way and run counter to our twenty-first-century sense of justice.

Some people, when they read the book, come away shaking their heads, struggling to harmonize the sometimes harsh pronouncements of Deuteronomy's God with the loving Savior-God portrayed in other biblical books.

But as you read through Deuteronomy, don't turn away. Don't give up on it. When you've finished all thirty-four chapters, I think you'll see that Deuteronomy, like the rest of the Bible, is a book about a God of grace.

> DIVINE MANDATES THAT RUB US THE WRONG WAY AND RUN COUNTER TO OUR TWENTY-FIRST-CENTURY SENSE OF JUSTICE.

A story I found on the Internet several years ago might help you understand why I can see a God of grace revealed in a book that seems focused more on laws and judgment than on forgiveness.

The story of Ugly the Cat has been out on the Internet for a long time, and you can read various versions of it and even see a YouTube version now. When I first read it more than a decade ago, it was attributed to Jennie Moss. Now it's usually posted as an anonymous story.

Somehow putting a name with the story helps make it real for me as an animal lover, so I like to picture someone named Jennie telling a story in which she personally had a part. Here's how she describes the cat that lived on the streets near her apartment.

> To start with, he had only one eye, and where the other should have been was a gaping hole. He was also missing his ear on the same side, his left foot appeared to have been badly broken at one time, and had healed at an unnatural angle, making him look like he was always turning the corner.
>
> His tail had long ago been lost, leaving only the smallest stub, which he would constantly jerk and twitch.
>
> Ugly would have been a dark gray tabby striped-type, except for the sores covering his head, neck, even his shoulders with thick, yellowing scabs. Every time someone saw Ugly there was the same reaction.
>
> "That's one UGLY cat!!"

Aside from his ugliness, the one thing that everyone noticed about Ugly was how much he craved love. He longed for someone to pick him up and pet him. He would rub up against legs whenever he got a chance, purring his heart out.

When children played outside, he would approach them and bump his head against their hands, hoping for a little pat, or that a youngster might be able to overlook his lack of beauty and rub behind his ears.

STILL THIS UGLY, MAIMED CREATURE CLUNG TO HOPE, ALWAYS COMING BACK TO GIVE A PERSON A SECOND CHANCE TO LOVE HIM.

But mostly he didn't get much affection. Mostly he got soaked by water hoses as adults tried to chase him away. Or he found himself dodging rocks that mean boys threw at him.

Still this ugly, maimed creature clung to hope, always coming back to give a person a second chance to love him.

But then one day Ugly offered his love to the wrong dog, and Jennie tells what happened next—and what she did—and how Ugly taught her a life-changing lesson. But before I share the rest of the story with you, let's make a personal application.

Can you empathize with Ugly the Cat?

Do you ever feel like that poor cat—unwanted, unloved, perhaps even ugly and undesirable? Have you ever been rejected—spurned by someone you only wanted to love you? Have you suffered the taunts of mean children or adults? Has someone important to you come out with a list of your shortcomings, reminding you over and over again just how faulty a person you are?

Most of us have suffered all of these pains at some time in our lives. Maybe you're going through an experience like that right now.

> DO YOU EVER FEEL UNWANTED, UNLOVED, PERHAPS EVEN UGLY AND UNDESIRABLE?

Maybe you've even made mistakes or committed sins that made you feel unworthy of God's love or anyone else's.

If you're ever tempted to feel unworthy of love, let me recommend a biblical book for you to read. It's called Deuteronomy.

Probably most people wouldn't think first of Deuteronomy if they were trying to suggest a book that would help someone who was discouraged and felt unloved. It's not one of the Gospels, after all. It's not a letter from Paul, who wrote about the greatest of gifts from God being love. It's not from John, who wrote the immortal words about how God so loved the world.

It's a book of sermons by Moses, the man we usually associate with laws, not love.

And, in fact, the book's very title, *Deuteronomy,* means "second law."

The title comes from the fact that after Israel had spent forty years wandering in the wilderness—because of their lack of faith in God—the Lord spoke through Moses and reminded the people of His commandments. He gave Israel His law a second time, in preparation for their move into the Promised Land.

So, you might be wondering, Ken, what makes you think a book of *laws* could help me feel better about myself? Laws usually make me feel worse about myself, because when I compare my life to the ideals

God has established, I get discouraged. Laws usually point out my problems; they don't help me feel better about myself!

It's a valid question: How can a *law* book help you when you're feeling discouraged or unworthy?

Well, that's where knowing the story behind the story helps.

This is why you hear the Voice of Prophecy recommend that people really dig in and thoroughly study the Bible as a whole book, instead of just memorizing a few proof texts or favorite passages. When you study the Book as a whole, you get the bigger picture of how God has worked with humanity throughout history. You can begin to see that the Bible is about journeys—about people on spiritual and physical journeys. And your exploration of the Bible becomes a genuine, amazing journey of its own.

> DEUTERONOMY IS ACTUALLY THE PRODUCT OF TWO *F*s: *FAILURE* AND *FORGIVENESS*.

When you understand the story behind—and around—the origin of the book of Deuteronomy, you begin to see this book of laws as a wonderful testimony to the love and patience of God.

Here's the amazing thing: Deuteronomy is actually the product of two *F*s: *Failure* and *Forgiveness*. The people's failure, and God's forgiveness.

In fact, the book would never have been written if it hadn't been for the failures and sins of God's people!

Deuteronomy preserves three sermons that Moses preached to the people of Israel as they prepared to move into Canaan *after* they had wandered for forty years in the wilderness because of their failure to trust God and go in and possess the Promised Land.

In these sermons, Moses shares God's laws with the people; but before he does that, he takes time to review their history—bringing up painful memories of how dastardly their deeds have been—how they failed to have faith and obey God's law in the past. Referring to their failure of faith when challenged to possess the land God had promised, Moses reminded them: "You were unwilling to go up; you rebelled against the command of the LORD your God. You grumbled in your tents and said, 'The LORD hates us; so he brought us out of Egypt to deliver us into the hands of the Amorites to destroy us' " (Deuteronomy 1:26, 27, NIV).

Several times throughout the book, Moses reminds the people of their past failures and admonishes them to be people of faith so that calamities will not come upon them in the future.

But Deuteronomy isn't all about fear, failings, and a foreboding future for the faithless. No, there's much more to it than that.

There are also many reminders of God's faithfulness—what He has already done for His people, and the good things He wants to bring into their lives—if only they will learn to trust Him.

In chapter 4, verses 36 and 37, Moses reminds them of how God both frightened them *and* declared His love for them at Mount Sinai: "From heaven he made you hear his voice to discipline you. On earth he showed you his great fire, and you heard his words from out of the fire. Because he loved your forefathers and chose their descendants after them, he brought you out of Egypt by his Presence and his great strength" (NIV).

Then, once again in chapter 7, Moses reaffirms that it is because God loves the people that He has brought them out of Egypt: "It was because the LORD loved you and kept the oath he swore to your forefathers that he brought you out with a mighty hand and redeemed you from the land of slavery, from the power of Pharaoh king of Egypt. Know therefore that the LORD your God is God; he is the faithful God, keeping his covenant of love to a thousand generations of those who love him and keep his commands" (verses 8, 9, NIV).

DESPITE THEIR REBELLIOUS WAYS, GOD HAS BEEN PATIENT WITH THEM.

Despite their rebellious ways, God has been patient with them. He hasn't abandoned them. He's continued to live among them and lead them. He's fed them manna, and He's even taken care of their clothes and shoes so that they didn't wear out for forty years!

In chapter 32, Moses breaks out into song to remind the people of God's goodness to them in calling them out of Egypt and leading them through the desert:

> I will proclaim the name of the LORD.
>   Oh, praise the greatness of our God! . . .
> For the LORD's portion is his people,
>   Jacob his allotted inheritance.

In a desert land he found him,
>   in a barren and howling waste.
He shielded him and cared for him;
>   he guarded him as the apple of his eye,
like an eagle that stirs up its nest
>   and hovers over its young,
that spreads its wings to catch them
>   and carries them on its pinions.
The LORD alone led him;
>   no foreign god was with him.
He made him ride on the heights of the land
>   and fed him with the fruit of the fields.
He nourished him with honey from the rock,
>   and with oil from the flinty crag,
with curds and milk from herd and flock
>   and with fattened lambs and goats,
with choice rams of Bashan
>   and the finest kernels of wheat.
You drank the foaming blood of the grape (Deuteronomy
>   32:3, 9–14, NIV).

And now, despite His children's failings, God is ready to give them a second chance. In Deuteronomy, He shares His laws—His rules for successful living—with them once again.

Oh, yes, the book of Deuteronomy is full of laws—lots of them—some of them a bit hard for us to understand or apply in the twenty-first century.

But it's also full of grace.

As you read, you may find it challenging to find the grace in some portions. Some of the laws demand harsh punishment for sin; others seem to let a person off with a slap on the wrist for things we consider abominable today.

> AFTER YOU FINISH READING THROUGH ALL THOSE LAWS AND PRONOUNCEMENTS, PLEASE NOTICE ONE THING.

But after you finish reading through all those laws and pronouncements, please notice one thing.

As the apostle Paul points out in the New Testament, it is "through the law [that] we become conscious of sin" (Romans 3:20). The law is like a mirror that God holds up in front of us, so we can look at ourselves and see how far from perfection we are. It allows us to see the wounds from old battles, the yellow scabs of sin festering on our souls.

God uses the law to help us realize how unworthy we are of His mercy. In Deuteronomy, He minces no words in telling His people just how badly they've failed, and even predicting how miserably they'll stumble in the future. But listen to what He says after all that:

"[W]hen you and your children return to the LORD your God and obey him with all your heart and with all your soul according to everything I command you to-

> IN SHORT, GOD SAYS TO HIS PEOPLE: I KNOW ALL ABOUT YOU.

day, then the LORD your God will restore your fortunes and have compassion on you. . . . He will bring you to the land that belonged to your fathers, and you will take possession of it. . . . Then the LORD your God will make you most prosperous in all the work of your hands and in the fruit of your womb, the young of your livestock and the crops of your land. The LORD will again delight in you and make you prosperous, just as he delighted in your fathers" (Deuteronomy 30:2–9, NIV).

In short, God says to His people, I know all about you. I know how weak you are, how easily you fall into sin. I see down into your hearts and see the ugliness of selfishness there. But I love you anyway. I know that your misdeeds will lead you into trouble and captivity. But I won't forget you. Wherever you are, when you turn back to Me, I'll be there for you!

And He still says the same to you today. Wherever you are, however rebellious you've been, He'll still be there for you if you'll return to Him.

> GOD IS IN THE BUSINESS OF RESCUING THE FALLEN.

Jennie Moss's story of Ugly the Cat has a sad, but poignant ending that in a way reminds me of the lesson of Deuteronomy.

One day Ugly got too close to a couple of dogs, and they beat him up really badly.

Now Jennie, unconcerned about appearances, ran to his rescue—but arrived too late.

Seeing him badly wounded, she scooped that ball of fur and puss and blood up in her arms and carried him to her apartment. And Ugly the Cat looked up into her eyes with love, and with his last breaths . . . began to purr out his adoration and love for her.

Maybe you sometimes feel a little ugly and unlovable; I know I do.

Maybe life has beat you up—or beat you down.

But you know what?

God is in the business of rescuing the fallen.

He wants to run to your aid and scoop you up in His arms, and—just as He did with Israel of old—give you another chance!

He's bending over you right now, wanting to help.

Won't you look up into His eyes right now and tell Him how much you love Him?

CHAPTER 6

Joshua: Conquering for God

Have you ever had a face-to-face encounter with God? Would you like to? How do you think you would respond? What, really, do you think it would be like to stand in the very presence of the Lord?

Do you think you would be like Isaiah, who cried out in alarm, "Woe is me! I am lost, for I am a man of unclean lips, and I live among a people of unclean lips; yet my eyes have seen the King, the LORD of hosts!" (Isaiah 6:5, NRSV)?

Or would you be like Moses, who turned aside one day to look at a burning bush that wasn't consumed, and suddenly heard a voice: " 'Moses, Moses! . . . Come no closer! Remove the sandals from your feet, for the place on which you are standing is holy ground.' . . . And Moses hid his face, for he was afraid to look at God" (Exodus 3:4–6, NRSV)?

> WE SHOULD NEVER LOSE SIGHT OF THE FACT THAT COMING INTO GOD'S PRESENCE IS A *PRIVILEGE*, NOT A RIGHT.

I hope you wouldn't be like Nadab and Abihu, sons of Aaron, who failed to properly respect the presence of the Lord and paid for it with their lives—or like Uzzah or King Uzziah, who suffered similar fates.

Christians know that we have the right to approach God's "throne of grace with boldness, . . . [and] receive mercy and find grace to help in time of need" (Hebrews 4:16, NRSV).

But we should never lose sight of the fact that coming into God's presence is a *privilege*, not a right. And that this privilege has been purchased at great expense through the gift of Jesus and His death on the cross.

It is a privilege given to us by God Himself. It's not something we should take for granted or presume upon lightly. The death of Jesus powerfully illustrates what every soul burdened with the weight of sin could expect to happen if he or she were to come into the presence of a Holy God unprotected by God's gracious gift of His Son.

Still, the Old Testament does give us several examples of people who were allowed to come face-to-face with God without dying. Which helps us to understand that God's grace was in action just as much in the Old Testament as in the New Testament.

Consider the case of Joshua, for example.

Joshua was a very old man when he encountered God face-to-face. The story is told in chapter 5 of the Bible book that bears his name.

For forty years Joshua had worked closely with Moses, leading God's people through trials, tribulations, and battles. Now the ancient warrior stood, looking across the dusty plain, facing his next obstacle—the fortified city called Jericho.

You've probably heard the song that says "Joshua fit the battle of Jericho . . . and the walls came a-tumbling down." As the old man stood that day, gazing at that city and its stone walls, he had never heard that song. He had only heard the command of the Lord to take the city as the first step in carving out a homeland for his people.

Joshua first appears in the Bible nearly forty years before this, as the commander of the army that defended Israel from the Amalekites at Rephidim. Here's the story as it's told in Exodus 17:

> AS THE OLD MAN STOOD THAT DAY, GAZING AT THAT CITY AND ITS STONE WALLS, HE HAD NEVER HEARD THAT SONG.

Moses said to Joshua, "Choose some men for us and go out, fight with Amalek. Tomorrow I will stand on the top of the hill with the staff of God in my hand." So Joshua did as Moses told him, and fought with Amalek, while Moses, Aaron, and Hur went up to the top of the hill. Whenever Moses held up his hand, Israel prevailed; and whenever he lowered his hand, Amalek prevailed. But Moses' hands grew weary; so they took a stone and put it under him, and he sat on it. Aaron and Hur held up his hands, one on one side, and the other on the other side; so his hands were steady until the sun set. And Joshua defeated Amalek and his people with the sword (Exodus 17:9–13, NRSV).

NOW, FORTY YEARS LATER, JOSHUA IS CHALLENGED TO "PUT HIS MONEY WHERE HIS MOUTH IS."

On that day Joshua had seen the power of the Lord and had learned to trust in his God—not in his own power—to defeat his enemies.

And he'd had to fight other battles along the way, as well. But prior to the stories we find in the book of Joshua, the battles had typically been defensive. Joshua had never been called upon to attack a fortified city before. He had captured some cities belonging to the Amorite king Sihon, but only after Sihon had attacked and Joshua had defeated his army *outside* the city.

Now, looking at the walls of Jericho, Joshua faced a major obstacle in fulfilling the mission God had given him.

But remember, from the stories in the book of Numbers, Joshua was an optimist, not a pessimist. When Moses sent him and eleven other men to spy out the land of Canaan, he and Caleb were the only ones who came back with an optimistic report.

When everyone else was saying that the land that God had promised to them was a land that devoured its people, and that it would devour them if they tried to take it, Joshua and Caleb said just the opposite: "The land we passed through and explored is exceedingly good. If the Lord is pleased with us, he will lead us into that land, a land flowing with milk and honey, and will give it to us. Only do not rebel against the Lord. And *do not be afraid* of the people of the land, because *we will swallow them up.* Their protection is gone, but the Lord is with us. Do not be afraid of them" (Numbers 14:7–9, NIV; emphasis added).

Notice the strong contrast here. The first group delivered the majority report: "The land we explored *devours* the people."

In their minority report, Caleb and Joshua turned the words back on their faithless compatriots: "Don't be afraid of those people. *We* will *swallow* them up!"

Now, forty years later, Joshua is challenged to "put his money where his mouth is"—to move forward in faith to conquer the land.

It's interesting, isn't it, that in preparation for the invasion, Joshua didn't send twelve spies to check out the land, he only sent two! Perhaps—after his experience forty years earlier—he figured that's all the opinions that anyone really needed! Forty years before, if Israel had listened to the two spies instead of the ten, they'd already be living in the Promised Land.

This time the spies bring back a positive prognosis: "Truly the LORD has given all the land into our hands; moreover all the inhabitants of the land melt in fear before us" (Joshua 2:24, NRSV).

People all over Canaan have heard stories about how the Lord delivered His people from slavery in Egypt, and it has literally put the fear of God into them.

But still, conquering a fortified city is no walk in the park.

Jericho's army is inside, waiting with arrows, spears, stones, and jars of boiling olive oil to pour on anyone who gets too close to the walls.

And so the old warrior stood, gazing at the walls shimmering in the heat rising from the floor of the Jordan Valley, not far from the Dead Sea—the lowest place on earth—and one of the hottest places!

And that's when God showed up. All his life, Joshua had fought the battles of God, walking by faith, not by sight.

But now he comes face-to-face with God. Joshua 5:13 says, "Once when Joshua was by Jericho, he looked up and saw a man standing before him with a drawn sword in his hand." At first, he doesn't know who this fearsome-looking man is, so he approaches him and asks, "Are you one of us, or one of our adversaries?" (NRSV).

> PERHAPS YOU'RE NOT ACCUSTOMED TO PICTURING GOD AS AN ARMED MAN WITH WEAPONS OF WAR IN HIS HANDS.

And then the story unfolds much like the story of Moses' encounter at the burning bush. The Lord identifies Himself as "commander of the army of the LORD," and Joshua—suddenly realizing whose Presence he is in, "fell on his face to the earth and worshiped, and he said to him, 'What do you command your servant, my lord?' The commander of the army of the LORD said to Joshua, 'Remove the sandals from your feet, for the place where you stand is holy.' And Joshua did so" (Joshua 5:14, 15, NRSV).

It's clear that it was not just an angel who appeared to Joshua, for an angel's presence would not make the ground holy. This is God Himself, come down to meet with Joshua and encourage him as he faces the toughest battle of his life.

Perhaps you're not accustomed to picturing God as an armed man with weapons of war in His hands. But it is God the warrior whom Joshua meets because he has been given a mission to fulfill: to carve out a place for God's people to live.

> THERE COMES A DAY WHEN A GOD OF LOVE MUST GO TO BATTLE, FOR HE CANNOT LET EVIL GO ON FOREVER.

Today, we seldom picture God with a sword in His hand. We prefer to focus on the love of God and the kindness of Jesus—and that has been the focus of our ministry at the Voice of Prophecy for more than eighty years.

But love isn't all satiny pillows and "butterfly kisses." Sometimes it has to take a firm stand in the conflict between right and wrong, good and evil.

This isn't just an Old Testament picture. Even Revelation, the last book of the New Testament, pictures Jesus coming to earth with a sharp sword coming out of His mouth! Personally I am a bit puzzled by the fact that when many of our modern Christian artists create pictures of Jesus riding down from heaven on a white horse, they almost never go the full distance in picturing what John the revelator described.

They put a friendly face on the Savior leading the charge against the forces of evil. But John saw Jesus charging forth on His white steed, fully armed for battle and with a sword protruding from His mouth! (See Revelation 19:11–16; compare Revelation 1:16; 2:12–16.)

There comes a day when a God of love must go to battle, for He cannot let evil go on forever.

And so in Joshua we find God with His sword in hand—preparing to do battle against those who will not accept His righteous rule. He strengthens Joshua's resolve to move forward—to go ahead with the difficult task of conquering the land.

And as Joshua bows down—falling right on his face in the dust of the place he is to conquer—God gives him a battle plan. One of the oddest battle plans ever enacted: "March around the city."

That's it.

March around the walls—just out of arrow-shot.

Do it over and over again, and let Me take care of the walls. Let Me knock down the obstacles that stand in your way.

We sing that "Joshua fit the battle of Jericho," but the truth is that God fought that battle for the people. God, not Joshua, knocked the walls down.

God gave His people a great victory, not because of their valor or skill in battle, but because of His faithfulness to His promise.

Jericho taught the people a lesson that they would need to remember as they went on to future battles. It is God's faithfulness, and their faith in Him, that brings victory. In the future battles that Joshua led the people into, there was only one defeat: the battle of Ai.

> GOD DIDN'T MISS A SINGLE THING. HE TRIED EVERY WAY IMAGINABLE TO WIN PEOPLE TO HIMSELF.

And if you remember that story, you know that this defeat came about because of the lack of faithfulness and obedience on the part of one of Joshua's soldiers, not because of the lack of faithfulness of the Lord.

After the cause of the failure at Ai had been identified and dealt with, God and Joshua led the people on to victory after victory. Under God's leadership, Joshua and the troops established a place where God's people could live and worship, free from outside influences and pressures to follow other gods.

The image of God we find in Joshua is the image of a Man with sword in hand, ready to give His people a place to live in security and freedom.

God has revealed Himself in different ways in different times. When Shakespeare wrote that "all the world's a stage," he wasn't far from the truth. When the great story of all the events of earth's history is finally summed up, we'll be able to look back over it all and see that God didn't miss a single thing. He tried every way imaginable to win people to Himself. Satan won't be able to accuse Him of not trying hard enough! For He's been willing to do whatever it would take to establish people in righteousness.

In an age of war and conquest, He made Himself known as the most powerful God of all.

But then, later, He came to earth again and walked the same ground as Joshua.

It's amazing, isn't it, to realize that the next time God Himself walked the earth at the crossing point of the Jordan, He appeared in a very different form—this time with no sword in His hand, but as the humble Lamb of God.

The Gospel of John describes it this way: "The next day [John the Baptist] saw Jesus coming toward him and declared, 'Here is the Lamb of God who takes away the sin of the world!' " (John 1:29, NRSV).

> THE NEXT TIME GOD HIMSELF WALKED THE EARTH AT THE CROSSING POINT OF THE JORDAN, HE APPEARED IN A VERY DIFFERENT FORM.

This time God came as a reconciler, not as a warrior. He came to unite all people's hearts in love to Him and to one another. He came to win the Promised Land not by combat, but by compassion. He came not to kill—but to die.

In each case He was at war—war for men's and women's hearts. For there is a war going on, and our God is willing to go to battle for us. At one time with hand outstretched, bearing a sword. At another time with hands outstretched, hanging from a cross.

In either case, He is our God, and He'll do what it takes to win—to win our hearts to Him. For that is what the battle is really about: winning hearts and saving souls.

And our part in the battle? Our part is the same as Joshua's: to welcome God's presence, to bow humbly before Him, and to follow His leading as we walk with Him by faith.

How would you respond if you were to come face-to-face with God? How would I respond?

I hope it would be like Joshua!

CHAPTER 7

Judges: When Religion Runs Amok

What does it mean to be a faithful servant of God? Obviously, there's more to it than just saying, "I have faith in God." When a person is called to serve God, there are certain expectations. But what if that person—or group of people—rebels and says, "I won't do it"?

The biblical book of Judges tells a series of stories about people like that.

And it illustrates—over and over again—what happens when people who are called to serve the Lord reject His claims on their lives. Story after story in the first sixteen chapters of Judges is built around the theme of what happens when people rebel and do not accept the calling of God to live as His servants.

Then the final five chapters tell additional stories about the mayhem that resulted when God's people didn't have adequate spiritual leadership, either in the form of following the Lord or following a king.

IT'S A STORY ABOUT A MAN WHOSE LIFE COULD HAVE TURNED OUT A LOT BETTER.

In the center of all these accounts is one of the most familiar stories in the whole Bible—in fact, one of the best-known stories in the world. It's been made into movies over and over again.

It has all the elements of an adventure, with—of course—a love triangle or two thrown in for good measure.

It's a story about a man—a very human man—whose life could have turned out a lot better, if only he hadn't rebelled against God's call. And it's a story about a man who was used by God in spite of himself.

It's the story of Samson.

It begins full of hope, but ends in a horribly tragic death. (But that's not really the end of the story, as we'll see in a moment.)

The story begins with hope because from the very get-go, Samson's life is a miracle. His mother was incapable of bearing children until one day an angel appeared to her and promised a son. But more than that, the angel promised that this son would grow up to fulfill a special mission: to deliver the people of Israel from oppression by the Philistines.

And that's where the story gets interesting.

Any good story needs to have conflict of some sort, we're told, to hold the reader's interest. The conflict throughout the story of Samson is between his own personal desires and God's desire to use him as a servant. This is where the question of being faithful to one's calling is played out. We all know the Samson story: how he struggled all his life against what must have seemed to him like the fetters of his calling.

> THE CONFLICT IS BETWEEN HIS OWN PERSONAL DESIRES AND GOD'S DESIRE TO USE HIM AS A SERVANT.

And yet in the end, he is listed in the book of Hebrews as a man of faith. Because in the end, he repented and submitted to be used as a servant of God.

The story of Samson comes down to us from the eleventh century B.C.—more than three thousand years ago! It comes to us from a time of war and disruption that affected the entire Mediterranean world. It's from the same time period as the famous story of the Trojan War.

In fact, historians now know that the Philistines arrived in Canaan somewhere around 1200 B.C. as part of a great migration of people that took place partly as a result of the Trojan War.

It was a time when people thought differently from the way we do today. In those times, most people thought that there were many gods in the world, lurking behind the scenes, influencing human events, and especially involving themselves in great, epic battles. Whichever nation's god was strongest would be the victor on the battlefield.

The Greek storytellers declared that the gods Athena, Hera, Poseidon, and Hermes had all fought on the Greek side against the Trojans. But God's people—the Israelites—knew (or at least should have known) that there is only one God ruling over the earth: the Lord, who had delivered their ancestors from slavery in Egypt.

> EVEN IN THE DIRE CIRCUMSTANCES THAT THEY BROUGHT UPON THEMSELVES, GOD DID NOT ABANDON THEM.

Unfortunately, as they entered into the Promised Land, the Israelites soon became sidetracked from their devotion to the God of their fathers. They forgot God and, as a result, found themselves in all kinds of trouble. Judges 2:11–15 introduces the motif that will be illustrated again and again in the stories that follow:

> The Israelites did what was evil in the sight of the LORD and worshiped the Baals; and they abandoned the LORD, the God of their ancestors, who had brought them out of the land of Egypt; they followed other gods, from among the gods of the peoples who were all around them, and bowed down to them. . . . So the anger of the LORD was kindled against Israel, and he gave them over to plunderers who plundered them, and he sold them into the power of their enemies all around, so that they could no longer withstand their enemies. Whenever they marched out, the hand of the LORD was against them to bring misfortune, as the LORD had warned them and sworn to them; and they were in great distress (NRSV).

But even in the dire circumstances that they brought upon themselves, God did not abandon them, as the next verse reveals: "Then the LORD raised up judges, who delivered them out of the power of those who plundered them" (verse 16).

These deliverers were called judges, not because they presided over a court of law, but because their job was to bring justice to God's people—to deliver them from their oppressors.

We hear—and talk—a lot about God being a God of love these

days, and sometimes when people read books such as Judges, they wonder if the Old Testament has a different God than the New Testament does. But believe me, when you're living under oppression, the greatest expression of love is deliverance. And in a world filled with violence, rebellion, and sin, the work of a deliverer all too often requires fighting fire with fire, matching forces of oppression sword-to-sword.

> WHEN YOU'RE LIVING UNDER OPPRESSION, THE GREATEST EXPRESSION OF LOVE IS DELIVERANCE.

The story of Samson is the story of one of the judges who was raised up to deliver God's people from their oppressors. But in a larger sense, the story of Samson is also the story of the entire people of Israel and their calling and their reaction to that call.

Samson's struggle against what God wanted him to do mirrors the attitude of the people he was sent to deliver. The story starts out this way: "The Israelites again did what was evil in the sight of the LORD, and the LORD gave them into the hand of the Philistines forty years" (Judges 13:1, NRSV).

When it came time to deliver His people from the Philistines, God had a plan, built around Samson. The Lord had great plans for Samson—so great, in fact, that He sent an angel to prepare his mother for his birth. You might even see some parallels to the Christmas story in this passage from Judges 13:

> There was a certain man of Zorah, of the tribe of the Danites, whose name was Manoah. His wife was barren, having borne no children. And the angel of the LORD appeared to the woman and said to her, "Although you are barren, having borne no children, you shall conceive and bear a son. Now be careful not to drink wine or strong drink, or to eat anything unclean, for you shall conceive and bear a son. No razor is to come on his head, for the boy shall be a nazirite to God from birth. It is he who shall begin to deliver Israel from the hand of the Philistines" (verses 2–5, NRSV).

Even before Samson was born, he was dedicated to the Lord to live a life of special purity as a Nazirite who would never drink wine or cut his hair. He was set aside by God for special purity—just as Israel had been set aside for special purity when God rescued the people from Egyptian bondage.

But when Samson grew up, he wanted nothing to do with his special vows. He was much more interested in getting married to a pretty Philistine girl—and *nobody* was going to stop him.

NO MAN COULD STOP HIM.
BUT A WOMAN COULD.

Because of God's special blessing, he was as strong as a dozen oxen, and nobody dared get in his way. When a lion attacked him, he tore it limb from limb. When his enemies tried to shut him up in a city, he ripped the gate off its posts and carried it away.

With God's blessing, he was like Israel back in the days of Joshua—strong and unstoppable.

But like his nation, his mind soon turned away from God to other things.

No man could stop him.

But a woman could.

First, it was the pretty Philistine girl. Then it was a prostitute from Gaza who almost got him killed. Finally, it was Delilah.

Love is blind, according to Shakespeare. And in Samson's case, love led ultimately to complete blindness. Delilah shaved his head and then, shorn of the symbol of his total devotion to God, Samson became as weak as any other man. The hero who had defeated a whole army with nothing but a donkey's jawbone for a weapon, now stood powerless before his enemies. They tied him up, put his eyes out, and put him to doing donkey's work grinding grain.

His eyes had always been his downfall—his weakest point—his Achilles' heel. But no more. Blinded and humiliated, Samson found himself in prison with a lot of time to think.

IT WAS THEIR OWN EYES THAT LED THE PEOPLE OF ISRAEL ASTRAY.

There's another phrase that runs like a refrain through the book of Judges. It's found in chapter 17, verse 6: "In those days there was no king in Israel; all the people did what was right *in their own eyes*" (NRSV; emphasis added).

It was his own eyes that led Samson astray. It was their own eyes that led the people of Israel astray.

The reason the Philistines were able to bind Samson was that God finally abandoned him to his own devices. The reason the Midianites, Ammonites, and others were able to defeat God's people was that they turned from Him, and He had to leave them to their own devices.

Too often it was only when they were defeated, blinded, and enslaved that they would finally turn back to God.

> WHEREVER YOUR EYES HAVE LED YOU, GOD STILL WANTS YOU.

Both the story of Samson and the book of Judges end with stories of victories won at great cost. Judges ends with a tragic story of warfare between the tribes of Israel. The tribe of Benjamin was nearly wiped out, and thousands of other Israelites died in the war as well. It was a war that could have been avoided if the people had remained true to God—had kept their eyes fixed on the purity He wanted for them. But in their blindness they wandered away from Him and into trouble that led to thousands of needless deaths.

For Samson, his greatest victory ever came when, in his despair, he finally gave himself wholeheartedly to God and cried out in utter dependence on God. At the end of his life, he brought down the temple of the Philistine god Dagon on top of his captors' heads. But that victory cost him his life.

Despite his failures along the way, Samson's name is found in the list of heroes of faith in Hebrews 11. In the end, he was willing to sacrifice all for his God to accomplish the task God had called him to do.

The book of Judges is a fascinating book—full of stories. It makes interesting reading. But perhaps its greatest lesson is found in this: though the people were not perfect, though God sometimes turned away from them, God never forsook them. He kept coming back, wooing them and winning them.

He does the same for us as well. Whatever your life story has been, wherever your eyes have led you, God still wants you. God still loves you. He wants you to turn back to Him. And He can still use you as a warrior in His kingdom.

CHAPTER 8

Ruth: Return to Promise

How do you handle the dry times in your life? The famines? The tough times?

Do you ever find yourself being tempted to abandon your faith and perhaps try some new strategies in life that don't involve God? Or strategies that perhaps replace God with other things? I think we all do from time to time.

Or is it possible that in your life God has just become less important to your daily walk. You slipped away from walking by faith, and gradually thoughts of God and living by faith have slipped away as well.

If that sort of thing has happened to you, you're certainly not alone. The Bible tells the story of one man to whom this happened. His name was Elimelech. Interestingly, his name means "My God is King!" But somehow he had come to the point where God wasn't really ruling in his life anymore.

> THERE'S ACTUALLY A MUCH RICHER REASON WHY THIS PARTICULAR STORY IS INCLUDED IN THE BIBLE.

Elimelech's faith situation is described very succinctly in Ruth 1:1: "In the days when the judges ruled, there was a famine in the land, and a certain man of Bethlehem in Judah went to live in the country of Moab, he and his wife and two sons" (NRSV).

Elimelech's life story could have been included in the book of Judges, I suppose. At least in its first few verses, the story makes much the same point as the stories in Judges: doing your own thing instead of walking by faith usually leads to disaster.

If the book of Ruth ended at verse 5 of the first chapter, we probably would conclude that it was just one more in a series of stories illustrating the folly of wandering away from the Lord.

There's actually a much richer reason why this particular story is included in the Bible—but you have to read clear to the end to discover it.

Elimelech appears to have been one of the people who, as Judges put it, "did what was right in his own eyes," without considering God's will. Or perhaps he was just a man in a desperate situation who decided to take matters into his own hands instead of walking by faith.

Did you ever watch the classic sitcom *Father Knows Best*? The plot, as I recall, usually revolved around some mischief or problem the kids got into, but by the end of the half hour things would have worked out OK because Father—Robert Young—would have come up with a solution, or the kids would have learned that they'd have been better off following Dad's advice in the first place.

IT'S A BOOK THAT MAKES THE WOMEN OUT TO BE THE SMART ONES IN THE FAMILY.

Today, we'd call a show like that "very '50s"—outdated and old-fashioned. Sitcom fathers don't fare as well at the hands of their script writers these days. Moms, or even the kids, are usually the ones who "know best," and the fathers' intellectual capacities are represented by Homer Simpson's oft-repeated "D'oh."

Well, believe it or not, that's not an entirely new concept. In fact, when you read the short four-chapter book called Ruth, you might conclude that it could have been titled "Mother Knows Best." It's a book that makes the women out to be the smart ones in the family—the ones who make the better choices.

If you've been told that the Bible is a male-chauvinistic book in which the men are always in charge and always saving the day, then I challenge you to read the book of Ruth. The second verse introduces Elimelech and his family this way: "The name of the man was Elimelech and the name of his wife Naomi, and the names of his two sons were Mahlon and Chilion; they were Ephrathites from Bethlehem in Judah. They went into the country of Moab and remained there" (NRSV).

Notice: It was Dad—Elimelech—who took his family over to

Moab to live. Things weren't going well in Bethlehem, and the word on the street was that things were better over on the other side of the Jordan River.

So Elimelech loaded up the family oxcart and took his wife, Naomi, and the two boys, and headed for Moab. And once the family was settled on that side of the Jordan, the boys married Moabite women.

It seemed like the move was a good idea—apparently, it was raining on the Moabite side of the river, but not on the Israelite side.

But, if you know your history, you might see a problem here that isn't obvious to the untrained eye.

If you understand the history of Israel and Moab, you recognize that Elimelech got things backward. The man's name means "My God is King," but he was moving his family away from Israel, where God was King, to Moab, a place where they worshiped a god they called Chemosh. We don't know a lot about this god, but one thing we do know is that he sometimes required human sacrifice. He was one of the gods that the Lord had told His people to beware of and never to worship.

> THIS WAS OUT-AND-OUT ABANDONMENT OF ONE RELIGION, ONE GOD, IN FAVOR OF ANOTHER.

In fact, when Israel was getting ready to move into the Promised Land, one of the worst crises they faced came about when Moabite women invited Israelite men to join in their religious festivals. Numbers 25:1, 2, says, "The people began to commit harlotry with the women of Moab. They [the Moabite women] invited the people to the sacrifices of their gods" (NKJV).

That detour into worshiping foreign gods led to disaster, with God commanding Moses to put to death many of the leaders of the people who had joined the Moabite women in worshiping Chemosh.

Now, some years later, when Elimelech moved his family from Bethlehem to Moab, he seemed to be falling into the same trap. He let his family be assimilated into the Moabite religion and race. He abandoned his God and his people in favor of Chemosh and the Moabites.

And his sons followed suit. They took Moabite women for their wives. This was no cross-denominational marriage, like a Presbyterian marrying a Lutheran. This was out-and-out abandonment of one religion, one god, in favor of another. And things did not work out well.

It wasn't long before Elimelech died. And a few years later, the two sons died. That left Mother—Naomi—home alone with two daughters-in-law.

Prospects for three widows in a male-dominated society didn't look good, and soon Naomi decided to head home—back to the land of her birth, back to the place where her God was worshiped.

> THAT'S WHY THERE IS A BIBLE BOOK NAMED AFTER RUTH, BUT NOT AFTER THE ONE NAMED ORPAH!

Both her daughters-in-law followed her part of the way, but when they came to a fork in the road, Naomi told them to go back home.

"Turn back, my daughters, why will you go with me? Do I still have sons in my womb that they may become your husbands? . . . No, my daughters, it has been far more bitter for me than for you, because the hand of the Lord has turned against me" (Ruth 1:11–13, NRSV).

One of her daughters-in-law, Orpah, did turn back. But not Ruth. And that's why there is a Bible book named after Ruth, but not after the one named Orpah!

When Naomi told Ruth to go back to her mother's house and worship Chemosh, Ruth responded with those familiar, heartwarming words that we often hear at weddings. They're found in Ruth 1:16, 17:

> But Ruth said:
>
> "Entreat me not to leave you,
> Or to turn back from following after you;
> For wherever you go, I will go;
> And wherever you lodge, I will lodge;
> Your people shall be my people,
> And your God, my God.
> Where you die, I will die,
> And there will I be buried.
> The LORD do so to me, and more also,
> If anything but death parts you and me" (NKJV).

What a choice Ruth had to make. It was the same sort of choice Elimelech had made years earlier. Elimelech's decision to abandon Israel and the God of his fathers in favor of Chemosh proved disastrous.

But Ruth's devotion to her mother-in-law and her choice to leave

Moab—to abandon Chemosh in favor of Israel's God Yahweh—proved to be right.

When Ruth and Naomi arrived in Bethlehem, Ruth continued to demonstrate her faithfulness and her strong character. Two widows living alone in Israel wouldn't necessarily have fared much better than widows in Moab. But they had two things going for them. They arrived at the beginning of the barley harvest, and Naomi had a secret that she hadn't yet shared with Ruth: there were relatives in town who just might prove helpful. In fact, there was the proverbial rich uncle.

Going back to Bethlehem wasn't an instant fix. Oh, no. Things didn't look good at all for the two women when they first arrived, penniless and homeless. Things looked so bad that Naomi, whose name means "delight," told people not to call her that anymore. "I've taken a new name," she said. "Don't call me Delight. Call me Bitter, because the Almighty has dealt very bitterly with me."

Maybe you've heard the adage "When life gets tough, it can make you either better or bitter." Well, we know from the story that life's challenges had made Naomi bitter.

BOAZ WAS THE "RICH UNCLE" THAT A WOMAN LIKE RUTH NEEDED TO MEET.

Fortunately, though, things were about to get better.

Naomi did the right thing by turning back to the Lord and returning to the Promised Land—the place where the Almighty could make things better, could "delight in her." And it wasn't long before Ruth met a fellow named Boaz.

Boaz was the "rich uncle" that a woman like Ruth needed to meet. He was a leading citizen in the town, and better yet, he was a close relative. Better still, when he saw Ruth, he liked what he saw.

Ruth was a hard worker; she went out into the fields where Boaz's servants were harvesting barley and began gathering up the few stalks of grain that they left behind. She was faithful—sharing what she gleaned with her mother-in-law.

Boaz watched her carefully and asked around about her. Other people had noticed her as well. Boaz told her, "All that you have done for your mother-in-law since the death of your husband has been fully told me, and how you left your father and mother and your native land and came to a people that you did not know before. May the LORD reward you for your deeds, and may you have a full reward from the LORD, the God of Israel, under whose wings you have come for refuge!" (Ruth 2:11, 12, NRSV).

Naomi, meanwhile, instructed Ruth exactly what to do in order that the two widows might find redemption.

That word *redemption* is an important word, based on the biblical concept of a kinsman-redeemer. That is, a close relative who could "bail you out," so to speak, if you got into financial difficulties and had to sell your land. The redeemer could pay your debts and buy your land back for you. And that's what Boaz did for Ruth.

IT TURNED OUT TO BE A *VERY* RIGHT DECISION. MOTHER, INDEED, KNEW BEST.

Elimelech's family still had rights to a piece of property, and the redeemer had the right to purchase that property, but it would also bring with it the responsibility of marrying the widow of the property's rightful owner.

Which would be Ruth.

So that's exactly what Boaz did. He took her place in court as a brother. He stood up for her. He paid her family's debts. And he reclaimed the inheritance that had originally belonged to her through marriage.

And he also took her as his bride.

He redeemed the poor, penniless, helpless widow, and made her the queen of his realm.

That's what the concept of the redeemer is all about in the Bible. That's what the story of Jesus coming to earth to purchase back the souls that have been lost to sin is all about. It's about Someone who loves you and me enough to take our debts and our sins upon Himself, and then claims us as members of His own family.

And in the story of Ruth, the fate of the two widows becomes even better. The last few verses of the book reveal that Ruth and Boaz had a son named Obed, and Obed had a son named Jesse, and Jesse had a son named David—King David, Israel's greatest king.

Ruth was David's great-grandmother!

And so, when Naomi chose to return to the Promised Land, to return to worshiping the God of Israel, it turned out to be a *very* right decision. Mother, indeed, knew best.

There's a lesson here in the book of Ruth for all of us, isn't there?

Our bad decisions all too often lead to bad results. We wander off into Moab, leaving God behind. But we can come back to Him; and when we do, He is still willing to be our Redeemer.

What Boaz did for Ruth reminds us of what Jesus wants to do for us as our Redeemer.

Friend, are you out in Moab today? Have you wandered away from God, let other things distract you—perhaps you've even become "married" to a false and fruitless way of life? Have things gone bad for you as you've turned your back on God?

It's not too late for you to make the Naomi choice—to turn back to God and let Him be your Redeemer.

CHAPTER 9

1 Samuel:
Looking for Leadership

If you want to know what the book of 1 Samuel is all about, consider its first story: the story of the birth of Samuel. It's a story about God hearing the plea of a barren woman and answering her prayer—giving her not just one son, but a whole flock of children: four sons and two daughters.

The name *Samuel* is commonly interpreted as "heard of God" or "asked of God," and time and again throughout the book the same thought is emphasized: God hears His people when they pray, and, in response, God's people are expected to listen when God speaks.

> ELI SEEMED UNCONCERNED AND WENT ABOUT BUSINESS AS USUAL. THE RESULTS WERE DISASTROUS.

Samuel is often the conduit of God's messages. People go to him asking for a word from the Lord, and he listens for the voice of God and shares it with the people.

When people listen and follow the advice of God, things go well for them. Those, however, who fail to hear the word of the Lord or fail to respond with obedience, soon find themselves in a world of hurt.

You've probably heard the story of how Samuel—as a young boy living at the tabernacle of God in Shiloh—heard the word of God. He shared the warning message that God gave him with the priest Eli, but Eli seemed unconcerned and went about business as usual. The results were disastrous for him, his family, and his nation.

Israel's first king, Saul, also failed to listen and properly heed the word of the Lord, and Samuel minced no words in pointing out the king's folly: "Samuel said to Saul, 'You have done foolishly; you have not kept the commandment of the LORD your God, which he commanded you. The LORD would have established your kingdom over Israel forever, but now your kingdom will not continue; the LORD has sought out a man after his own heart; and the LORD has appointed him to be ruler over his people, because you have not kept what the LORD commanded you' " (1 Samuel 13:13, 14, NRSV).

THE TIMES WE REMEMBER BEST ARE OFTEN TIMES THAT WE WOULDN'T WANT TO LIVE THROUGH AGAIN.

Samuel's rebuke states succinctly the theme of this Bible book: when God speaks, man's role is to listen and respond. God is no respecter of human rank or pride. Our role, no matter how important we may think we are, is to humbly listen for God's guidance and follow it.

First Samuel is one of the most interesting books in the Old Testament—full of exciting stories that we like to tell to children: Samuel in the sanctuary, hearing God's voice, David and Goliath, the call and anointing of a shepherd boy to be king of Israel, Jonathan's daring exploits against the Philistines, David and Saul in the cave, and the way David spared Saul's life not once but twice!

It was an exciting, but stressful, time to be living.

Have you noticed that about life? The times we tell stories about— the times we remember best—are often times that we wouldn't want to live through again. Times when we faced a special challenge, or perhaps prayed our way out of a life-threatening situation.

First Samuel tells plenty of those kinds of stories.

There's a reason these stories of conflict and war are in the Bible. Most of us are familiar with the verse in Paul's first letter to the members of the church he had founded in Corinth, in which he sought to help them grasp the importance of understanding these Old Testament stories.

"Now these things which happened to our ancestors are illustrations of the way in which God works, and they were written down to be a warning to us who are the heirs of the ages which have gone before us" (1 Corinthians 10:11, Phillips).

Paul was concerned that the new Christians at Corinth were failing to heed the word of the Lord, just as the children of Israel had done in their trek through the wilderness, and he didn't want his friends to suffer the same sort of fate.

I know that many Christians are troubled by some of the stories they find in the Old Testament, and some have even told me they don't read the Old Testament anymore—they'd rather focus on the ministry of Jesus in the Gospels. But Paul wanted the Corinthians—and us—to know that these stories are important to our understanding of God.

We can learn from the stories and avoid the pitfalls that men such as Saul and Eli and their ancestors fell into.

There really are some important things to be learned by reading the history recorded in 1 Samuel and other Old Testament books. So, as we approach these stories, let's look for the core. Let's look for the lesson we're supposed to learn. The central lesson comes through loud and clear if you do a careful read of one of the early stories, found in chapter 4.

It was a time of severe crisis. A time when men hang their heads in shame and wondered, Where is God in all of this?

Four thousand Israelite men lay dead on the fields near Aphek—a strategically located village on the border between Philistine territory and Israelite territory.

The Philistines had massed their armies at Aphek, planning an assault along a major road that led right into the heart of Israelite territory—right up to the area where the ark of God's covenant was kept at Shiloh.

The Israelites, sensing imminent doom, had rallied across the valley from them, hoping to cut them off at the pass. But when the battle commenced, the Israelite army met with disaster.

And in the evening, the defeated, demoralized, humiliated army hunkered down around their cooking fires and asked themselves what had gone wrong. Why would God allow them to suffer such a defeat?

And in this story, told in 1 Samuel 4, we find a powerful illustration of the central, core message of the entire book. The lesson becomes obvious in two things: what the men didn't do, and what they did do.

THE CENTRAL LESSON COMES THROUGH LOUD AND CLEAR IF YOU DO A CAREFUL READ OF ONE OF THE EARLY STORIES.

Over and over, throughout this book, those who do not inquire of the Lord, those who do not hear—or do not listen to—the word of the Lord, go down in defeat.

Samuel is the great leader of Israel who hears God's voice and reveals God's will.

> IT SEEMS LIKE WE'RE PROGRAMMED FROM THE CRADLE TO BLAME OURSELVES WHENEVER SOMETHING GOES WRONG.

But in the story in chapter 4, when the army suffered defeat, notice that they didn't ask Samuel to inquire of the Lord as to why they had been defeated. According to verse 3, the elders of the people inquired among themselves, asking themselves questions, such as, "What could we have done differently? How can we get God to bless us?"

Perhaps the advice that we find in Proverbs 3:5–8 hadn't yet been written down; nonetheless, the men should have realized the importance of this principle:

> Trust in the LORD with all your heart,
> And lean not on your own understanding;
> In all your ways acknowledge Him,
> And He shall direct your paths.
> Do not be wise in your own eyes;
> Fear the LORD and depart from evil.
> It will be health to your flesh,
> And strength to your bones (NKJV).

Unfortunately, in this instance the army of Israel "leaned on their own understanding." Don't miss that point.

And what was it that they *didn't* do? They didn't ask God's guidance. They didn't listen for the word of the Lord. They simply asked themselves what they had done wrong.

It's easy to fall into that trap, isn't it? It seems like we're programmed from the cradle to blame ourselves whenever something goes wrong—to kick ourselves with questions such as, "Why am I so stupid—why did I let this happen—why didn't I . . . ?" It's natural to think that if we'd only made better decisions things would have turned out better.

But in the story we're looking at, the problem wasn't just a matter of making wrong choices. There was a spiritual problem at the root of their defeat. The problem wasn't with how the army marched; it wasn't a matter of one of the generals retreating when he should have advanced. The problem was with the people's relationship to God and their trust in Him.

But when they tried to solve the problem—when they finally resorted to putting their faith in God—they still didn't get it right.

Oh, yes, they seemed to repent and turn to God—on the surface it seemed as if they were doing all the right things. They decided that what they needed was God's help. Not a bad decision in itself. But notice how they went about trying to get God's help: "When the troops came to the camp, the elders of Israel said, 'Why has the LORD put us to rout today before the Philistines? Let us bring the ark of the covenant of the LORD here from Shiloh, so that he may come among us and save us from the power of our enemies' " (1 Samuel 4:3, NRSV).

HAVE YOU EVER DONE THAT? DEMANDED THAT GOD COME AND MEET YOU ON YOUR TERMS, IN YOUR PLACE, AT YOUR TIME?

Coming up with their own answers and solutions, they sent messengers running up to Shiloh, where the tabernacle of God was, and they had the priests carry the ark of the covenant—God's holy dwelling place on earth—down to the battlefield.

Now, at first glance, that seems like a pretty good idea. If God is in the camp with them, how can they be defeated?

But think for a moment about what's really happening here.

Is God leading the people, or are the people leading God? Who's in charge here? Who's on the throne?

That's the question.

Let me tell you about Neil.

Neil was a big, burly fellow. He looked like he could go into the ring with an Olympic wrestler and come out OK. He was an ex-con, a professional safecracker, who'd reformed. He'd met Jesus in prison, and come out singing the praises of God.

He was the kind of guy who would load up his car with Christian tracts and books and go down to the roughest neighborhoods of Milwaukee, Wisconsin, and fearlessly share his faith with drug pushers and loan sharks.

But after a time, he began to lapse back into his old ways. He got discouraged and lost touch with God—began to doubt his conversion experience. When I, as his pastor, went by to visit, Neil looked me in the eye, and said, "Pastor, if there's a God in heaven, I want to see Him. I want Him to come right down here—sit right in that chair, and talk to me!"

Have you ever done that? Demanded that God come and meet you on your terms, in your place, at your time?

Do we sometimes—just maybe—do that in the way we pray? In the way that we demand that God "fulfill His promises" in just the way we want Him to? And then when we don't get our way, we blame God, or we question Him—maybe even question whether there is a loving God in heaven.

Is it just possible your faith has suffered, grown weak, because God hasn't let you dictate what He'll do, and when He'll do it?

That's what happened to Israel at Aphek. They didn't ask for God's leadership. They tried to pick up God and carry Him into battle with them. And it didn't help their cause at all. They still went down in defeat. There was a massive slaughter that day—far worse than what had happened the day before. The Israelite soldiers that survived went running home, utterly overthrown—powerless to resist the onslaught. And the Philistines marched into the hills, burning and pillaging the Israelite villages and strongholds.

Worse yet, the Philistines captured the ark of the covenant—the symbol of God's presence on earth.

> ISRAEL'S ARMY MAY HAVE BEEN DEFEATED, BUT ISRAEL'S GOD HAD NOT!

But if you know the rest of the story, you know what happened next. God was fully able to take care of Himself—of His ark of the covenant. The Philistines soon learned that the God of Israel was more powerful than their gods—even if the Israelite army was no match for theirs right then. After they captured the ark, the Philistines took it down to one of their chief cities, Ashdod, and they put it in the temple of their god Dagon.

It seemed like a natural thing to do. In those days people assumed that if their armies were victorious in battle, it meant that their god was stronger than the god of the people they had defeated.

But boy, did the Philistines have a lesson to learn. Israel's army may have been defeated, but Israel's God had not!

The next morning when the priests went into the temple, they found the statue of their god flat on his face, bowing to the God of Israel.

"*Humpf,* must have been a minor earthquake last night," they said, and they set their god up again. Next morning though, he'd fallen on his face again, and his head and hands had broken off! Israel's God had not been defeated!

And go on from that story. Read the rest of the book of 1 Samuel. Notice how often the man who emerges as its hero—David—appeals to God for guidance. Notice how Saul and others succeed when they listen to God, but fail when they don't listen.

There's a powerful lesson here for us—a powerful admonition. Listen for the voice of God in your life. Look for God's leading in His Word. And be willing to respond.

When you're tempted to drag God into the situation you face, to demand that He fight your battles for you, be sure to check first: whose idea is this—God's or mine? God is well able to deliver—you, and Himself. But I think it was Abraham Lincoln who pointed out that when it comes to battles, the question is not whether God is on my side—but whether I'm on His.

Who's in charge here? Who's on the throne in your life?

CHAPTER 10

2 Samuel: The Perils of Power

The commotion in Jerusalem was earth-shattering.

Possession of the city of Jerusalem is an issue that can shake the world even today.

But the story we're looking at today happened nearly three thousand years ago. Already then, there was a dispute over who should live there, whose capital it should be.

It was known as King David's city. He and his troops had conquered it a quarter century earlier. But right in the middle of the book of 2 Samuel, we find the city in tumult. The story is told in chapter 15.

Absalom, one of David's sons, had been working behind the scenes to turn people against his father, and to set himself up as the new candidate for the throne. After years of subterfuge, he had himself proclaimed king in David's former capital city, Hebron.

AS WE EXPLORE THIS STORY AND THE BOOK OF 2 SAMUEL, WE'LL DISCOVER WHAT'S BEHIND HIS DECISION.

Meanwhile, back in Jerusalem, a messenger came running up to David with the news that Absalom was marching on the city with a large army. Notice David's response. It seems odd, but as we explore this story and the book of 2 Samuel, we'll discover what's behind his decision.

"Then David said to all his officials who were with him at Jerusalem, 'Get up! Let us flee, or there will be no escape for us from Absalom. Hurry, or he will soon overtake us, and bring disaster down upon us, and attack the city with the edge of the sword' " (2 Samuel 15:14, NRSV).

So the renowned warrior-king David took the servants who remained faithful to him and hastily packed a few provisions on the backs of donkeys and hurried out of town, heading for the far side of the Jordan River.

WHY WOULD KING DAVID, THE MAN WHO FOUGHT SO MANY BATTLES FOR GOD, LEAVE THE CITY LIKE A SCARED RABBIT?

What a strange reaction. Why would King David, the man who fought so many battles for God, leave the city like a scared rabbit running from a wolf?

Running from his own son—what would make him do that?

Well, for one thing, David realized that what was happening to him was God's righteous judgment on him.

When you think of David, you probably think of the phrase "He was a man after God's own heart."

We tend to paint halos around heroes like that, don't we? Thinking of them as paragons of virtue who always lived out their faith in God.

But, of course, we know better than that about David.

We've all heard the story of David and Bathsheba.

Yes, David was known as a man after God's own heart. But he still had his failings. God blessed him with a kingdom and great power. Sometimes blessings are harder to handle than difficulties and disasters. Sometimes it's the blessings that trip us up in our walk with God.

When we begin to take them for granted.

When we begin to think that God has blessed us because we are good and righteous and strong.

When we start letting the success God has given us go to our heads.

It happened to David. He became a victim of the perils of power. He let his power go to his head.

He got to the point where he seemed to believe it was his right to take any man's wife for his own. And if the man wouldn't cooperate, he knew how to handle that situation too.

In the case of Bathsheba, he had her husband—a faithful soldier who was listed among the top thirty warriors of his nation—killed in battle!

Power had gone to David's head, and it formed a corrupting

82

coalition with lust in his heart; then one thing led to another, then another, until "good" King David had committed murder.

After this sin, which David thought he got away with scot-free, the prophet Nathan came to him and told him a story that brought him up short. Nathan told him about a wealthy man who cruelly took away the one lamb that belonged to a poor man instead of sacrificing one of his own lambs to feed his guests.

On hearing this story, "David's anger was greatly kindled against the man. He said to Nathan, 'As the LORD lives, the man who has done this deserves to die; he shall restore the lamb fourfold, because he did this thing, and because he had no pity' " (2 Samuel 12:5, 6, NRSV).

> HE REALIZED THAT WHAT WAS HAPPENING TO HIM NOW WAS PART OF THE JUDGMENT THAT NATHAN HAD PREDICTED.

Once he'd gotten David's reaction, Nathan looked the king square in the eye, and stated: "You are the man! Thus says the LORD, the God of Israel: I anointed you king over Israel. . . . I gave you your master's house, and your master's wives into your bosom, and gave you the house of Israel and of Judah. . . . Why have you despised the word of the LORD, to do what is evil in his sight? You have struck down Uriah the Hittite with the sword, and have taken his wife to be your wife, and have killed him with the sword of the Ammonites. *Now therefore the sword shall never depart from your house,* for you have despised me, and have taken the wife of Uriah the Hittite to be your wife" (verses 7–10, NRSV; emphasis added).

So, one of the reasons why David fled from Jerusalem instead of standing to fight against his son Absalom was that he realized that what was happening to him now was part of the judgment that Nathan had predicted would come upon him for his sin.

He recognized that his throne and his city were gifts from God. They belonged to him only because of the grace of God that had taken him from being a humble shepherd boy and placed him on the throne of Israel.

And if there is one sterling characteristic of David that comes through in almost all the stories of his life, it is his trust in God and his surrender to the will of God. Even when he sinned, even when he failed God miserably, still he trusted.

When he came to his senses, this man of God always cast himself upon the mercy of God.

You don't find him making excuses or trying to justify himself. He just admits his sin and asks forgiveness.

One of the best-loved psalms in all the Bible is Psalm 51, David's penitent prayer, asking forgiveness for his great sin in the matter of Bathsheba.

> Have mercy on me, O God,
> according to your steadfast love;
> according to your abundant mercy
> blot out my transgressions.
> Wash me thoroughly from my iniquity,
> and cleanse me from my sin.
> For I know my transgressions,
> and my sin is ever before me.
> Against you, you alone, have I sinned,
> and done what is evil in your sight,
> so that you are justified in your sentence
> and blameless when you pass judgment. . . .
> Create in me a clean heart, O God,
> and put a new and right spirit within me.
> Do not cast me away from your presence,
> and do not take your holy spirit from me (Psalm 51:1–4,
> 10, 11, NRSV).

David was fully aware of his sin and of his responsibility for bringing this tragic civil war upon his nation.

Now, notice what happened as David and his household were hurrying out through the gates and down into the valley, on their way to a life of homelessness.

Zadok, the priest of God, followed David out of the city, bringing the ark of the covenant of God with him!

> HE WANTED DAVID TO BE SURE TO TAKE GOD WITH HIM TO GIVE HIM VICTORY!

He wanted David to take the ark with him out into the wilderness.

He wanted David to be sure to take God with him to give him victory!

Now stop just a moment.

What was the lesson we took away from the book of 1 Samuel?

Let's just take a quick refresher course. Remember, before David's time, when the Israelites were being defeated by the Philistines. What did they do?

They went to Shiloh, picked up the ark, and took it with them into battle.

But did it solve their problem?

No.

Why not?

Because they were trying to take God with them. They were trying to press God into service in their cause, rather than surrendering to God's will and letting Him lead them.

They had it all backward.

Think back to the stories from the time when God was leading Israel through the wilderness for forty years. Whenever they would set out on their journey, the ark of the covenant of the Lord went *before* them. The people were to follow God's leading. God was not to follow their lead.

> WE FORM A GREAT STRATEGIC PLAN AND THEN WE SAY, "WELL, LET'S SAY A PRAYER AND ASK GOD TO BLESS US."

We still get that backward sometimes today, too, don't we? We know what we want to accomplish. We lay great plans for getting from point A to point B. Whether it's in our individual lives or in the plans we lay for our churches.

We form a great strategic plan and get ready to move forward. And then we say, "Well, let's say a prayer and ask God to bless us in what we're going to do."

Wouldn't it be better if we prayed *before* we laid our plans? Wouldn't it be better if we let God guide us as we laid our plans instead of expecting God to work within our plans? Figuratively picking up the ark and dragging it along behind us as we go the way we've chosen!

There's something we can learn from David here. As he was fleeing from Jerusalem, he was confronted with the temptation to do just what the people had done a few years earlier—drag the ark into the battle—demand that God come and fight on his side.

It was fully within his power to take the ark with him.

But did he do it? Would he press God into his service—tell the Lord of the universe where to go and what to do? The answer is found in 2 Samuel 15:24–26: "Abiathar came up, and Zadok also, with all the Levites, carrying the ark of the covenant of God. They set down the ark of God, until the people had all passed out of the city. Then the king said to Zadok, 'Carry the ark of God back into the city. If I find favor in the eyes of the LORD, he will bring me back and let me see both it and the place where it stays. But if he says, "I take no pleasure in you," here I am, let him do to me what seems good to him' " (NRSV).

Would David compel God to come with him into battle? Or would David surrender to God's will? That was the question.

As far as running ahead of God, as far as taking matters into his own hands, David had been there, done that. That's what he had done in the matter of Bathsheba and her husband Uriah the Hittite. And it had brought them nothing but trouble—specifically the trouble he was in right then.

> HE KNEW THAT NOW IT WAS TIME TO ENTRUST HIMSELF INTO GOD'S HANDS, RATHER THAN TAKING GOD INTO HIS HANDS.

He'd had enough of that. He knew that now it was time to entrust himself into God's hands, rather than taking God into his hands.

So David told Zadok to take the ark back into the city.

And he committed himself into God's care and keeping.

That's something David had learned to do through years of experience that taught him to trust in his God. And if you know the rest of the story, you know that God honored his decision, gave him victory, and brought him back to Jerusalem as king.

A phrase that occurs again and again is "David inquired of the LORD." David asked God what to do, instead of telling God what he wanted done.

The book of 2 Samuel is full of fascinating stories. In some places, it reads almost like a romance novel; in others, a war diary. It's a story about a man and his family—and especially about learning to know and trust God.

David was not perfect. But we can learn from him.

What is your kingdom like today? Is it peaceful and prosperous, or filled with temptations of the flesh? Now is the time to be on guard. Don't be a victim of the perils of power as David was.

Or is your world full of conflict? Is someone trying to "steal your throne" right out from under you? David's story can teach you how to handle that as well. Entrust yourself into God's care every day. Don't give up. Even when the Philistines—or your own family—are on the attack and everything seems hopeless, He will be there for you. Even in your weakest hour, He will be strong for you.

CHAPTER 11

1 Kings: More Perils of Power

I f only I had known, I should have become a watchmaker."

Those are the words of a wise man, looking back over his life, wondering whether he had done the right thing with his time and talent. He was a man whose mind had grasped great things in ways that seemed improbable, if not impossible, to others. He had a unique way of looking at the world around him—right down to the very core of things.

As word of his unique ideas spread, he became famous all over the world. By the end of his life, he was so famous that prior to his death, he made special arrangements to have his body cremated and his ashes spread to the four winds. He didn't want his grave to become a shrine for curiosity seekers. But a physician, fascinated by what made this man such a genius, stole his brain and preserved it, and researchers still ponder it today, seeking clues as to what made this man so uniquely brilliant.

And yet this wise man, this famous man—with one of the most widely recognized faces in all the

HIS FAMOUS VISAGE GAZED OUT LIKE SOME SORT OF DEITY AMID A FIELD OF STARS ON THE COVER OF THE FIRST ISSUE OF *TIME* MAGAZINE IN THE YEAR 2000.

world, looking back over his life, said in all candor, *If I had it all to do over again, I would have done things differently—I would have become a watchmaker—I would have stayed in a little village in Switzerland, unknown to the outside world, and applied my great intellect to the task of making the finest watches possible.*

By now you've probably figured out who I am referring to.

His famous visage, with its wild, silver mane, gazed out like some sort of deity amid a field of stars on the cover of the first issue of *Time* magazine in the year 2000. "Person of the Century," they called him. Because, at least in the opinion of the editors of *Time,* the things Albert Einstein figured out changed our world more than anything anyone else thought up in the entire hundred years.

They credited him with changing the world more than national leaders such as Franklin Roosevelt, Winston Churchill, Mahatma Gandhi, and Mao Tse-tung.

They felt his ideas had more of an impact than megalomaniacal, death-dealing dictators such as Stalin and Hitler.

Great warriors such as Eisenhower, Montgomery, Patton, Yamamoto, and Rommel were deemed to have changed the world less by their *actions* than Einstein did by his *thinking*!

> IF HE COULD HAVE A DO-OVER, HE WOULD SPEND HIS LIFE TINKERING WITH TINY COGS AND GEARS.

And yet, looking back over his life, Einstein had regrets. He said that if he could have a do-over, he would spend his life tinkering with tiny cogs and gears in a watch shop instead of tampering with the fundamental building blocks of the universe.

It was Albert Einstein, you see, whose ideas unlocked the door of the nuclear age, unleashing upon the world the greatest power known in the physical realm.

But what troubled him, I think, is that where there is great power, there is also great peril.

Einstein opened the door to great power but also to great peril. And in the end, he decided that perhaps it would have been better if he had not thought the great thoughts that changed our world.

Albert Einstein was, of course, not the only person to look back over his life and muse, "What if I had done things differently?"

Here are the words of another wise man who looked back over his life with some regrets: "I have seen all the things that are done under the sun; all of them are meaningless, a chasing after the wind" (NIV).

And if he had left it at that, it would be a dismal picture of the world indeed, but this wise man dared to go deeper, to explore the meaning of life with even greater wisdom; and in the end, he gave us this erudite assessment of what life is all about: "Now all has been heard; here is the conclusion of the matter: Fear God and keep his commandments, for this is the whole duty of man" (NIV).

These, of course, are the words of Israel's wise king, Solomon, found in Ecclesiastes 1:14 and 12:13 (in other words, at the beginning and the end of the book of Ecclesiastes).

So how wise was Solomon? Well, if *Time* magazine had been around three thousand years ago, I have a feeling that King Solomon might have been voted "Person of the Century" at the end of the tenth century B.C.

Here's the biblical testimony of just how great this man was: "God gave Solomon wisdom and exceedingly great understanding, and largeness of heart like the sand on the seashore. Thus Solomon's wisdom excelled the wisdom of all the men of the East and all the wisdom of Egypt. For he was wiser than all men . . . ; and his fame was in all the surrounding nations. He spoke three thousand proverbs, and his songs were one thousand and five. . . . And men of all nations, from all the kings of the earth who had heard of his wisdom, came to hear the wisdom of Solomon" (1 Kings 4:29–34, NKJV).

> KING SOLOMON MIGHT HAVE BEEN VOTED "PERSON OF THE CENTURY" AT THE END OF THE TENTH CENTURY B.C.

Certainly he could have been named the person of his century, don't you think? He lived and reigned in great power.

But the question is, In handling such power, did he avoid falling into its pitfalls and perils?

Solomon's reign began well, with his prayer for wisdom, found in 1 Kings 3. As a young man he recognized his weakness and need of divine guidance: "And now, O LORD my God, you have made your servant king in place of my father David, although I am only a little child; I do not know how to go out or come in. And your servant is in the midst of the people whom you have chosen, a great people, so numerous they cannot be numbered or counted. Give your servant therefore an understanding mind to govern your people, able to discern between good and evil; for who can govern this your great people?" (1 Kings 3:7–9, NRSV).

The next thing we read about Solomon in 1 Kings is the story of the two women who were arguing over whose baby had died during the night and whose baby had survived, and Solomon's crafty way of figuring out who the real mother was.

Several chapters of the book detail preparations for building the temple of the Lord, the construction process, and a list of the rich furnishings that Solomon provided for it—including many items made of gold or plated with gold.

Chapter 8 shares the prayer that Solomon offered on the day the temple was dedicated and his recognition that though he had built a house for God to dwell in, no human construction could ever truly contain God: "Will God indeed dwell on the earth? Even heaven and the highest heaven cannot contain you, much less this house that I have built!" (1 Kings 8:27, NRSV).

> SOLOMON STARTED OUT WELL, CONSULTING GOD AND APPEALING FOR GOD'S GRACE.

Solomon went on to pray for his people and to ask that God would honor the temple. Knowing his people's propensity for rebelling and falling into disaster (remember our study of the book of Judges), Solomon asked that if the people would pray at this place, that God would answer their prayers.

When the book of 2 Chronicles tells the story of Solomon's prayer, it includes God's answer, which has been turned into a well-known song: "I have heard your prayer, and have chosen this place for myself as a house of sacrifice. . . . If my people who are called by my name humble themselves, pray, seek my face, and turn from their wicked ways, then I will hear from heaven, and will forgive their sin and heal their land" (2 Chronicles 7:12–14, NRSV).

So Solomon started out well, consulting God and appealing for God's grace. His story takes up nearly half of the book of 1 Kings. He reigned for forty of the 220 years covered, and this Bible book has much to say in praise of his early reign. Unfortunately, though, the old adage that power corrupts proved true even for Solomon. The perils of power soon got the best of him, and though he was known among the kings of the earth as the wisest, he soon succumbed to follies like a child set loose in a candy store. His folly wasn't sweets, though. It was "sweeties"! By the time he was done, he had married hundreds of women and taken hundreds of concubines.

Some of these marriages, such as marrying the daughter of Pharaoh, were, no doubt, political—to cement alliances with powerful neighbors. But as we'll notice later, even that crafty move toward alliance with Egypt eventually ended in disaster.

Worst of all, in order to maintain his lavish lifestyle, he enslaved many of the people of Israel, forcing them into hard labor.

When Solomon died, his son Rehoboam took the throne and had an opportunity to distance himself from some of his father's excesses. The leaders asked him to relax the slave-labor levy. But Rehoboam refused, and a long civil war ensued. The kingdom of Israel was split in two, with Rehoboam ruling only two tribes—forming the kingdom of Judah—while ten tribes formed what came to be known as the kingdom of Israel.

> EVEN THAT CRAFTY MOVE TOWARD ALLIANCE WITH EGYPT EVENTUALLY ENDED IN DISASTER.

The book of 1 Kings contains many more stories; for instance, a series of stories about the prophet Elijah. The story of Elijah on Mount Carmel, when he challenged the prophets of Baal to have their god—who was considered to be the god of lightning and thunder—bring fire down from heaven.

I like the way the Jerusalem Bible translates Elijah's speech to the people of Israel at that time: "How long . . . do you mean to hobble first on one leg then on the other? If Yahweh is God, follow him; if Baal, follow him" (1 Kings 18:21).

It is also in 1 Kings that we read of Elijah's run to Mount Horeb and his experience there when he learned that God is not in the earthquake or the storm, but in the still, small voice speaking to the conscience.

Another story that captures the spirit—the entire message—of 1 Kings, comes just a few years after the death of Solomon.

Solomon, you see, was very wise. But he wasn't wise enough to continue to follow the Lord's leading all through his life. He didn't follow his own counsel found in Proverbs 3:

> HE LEARNED THAT GOD IS NOT IN THE EARTHQUAKE OR THE STORM, BUT IN THE STILL, SMALL VOICE.

Trust in the LORD with all your heart,
And lean not on your own understanding;

In all your ways acknowledge Him,
And He shall direct your paths (verses 5, 6, NKJV).

In all his enthusiasm for doing great things, he overstepped his bounds, abused the power entrusted to him, and put heavy burdens on his people, which led to civil war and the breakup of the kingdom.

And even Solomon's politically strategic marriages ended up backfiring, because events in Egypt were chaotic in his day. The powerful twentieth dynasty had ended a century before Solomon took the throne in 971 B.C., and Egypt had entered a time of turmoil known to historians as the Third Intermediate Period.

Egypt's twenty-first dynasty lasted only from 1069 until 945 B.C. History tells us that in the middle of Solomon's forty-year reign, the last pharaoh of the twenty-first dynasty was replaced on the throne by his military chief of staff, Sheshonq. The new pharaoh founded the twenty-second dynasty, reigning as Sheshonq I. With the change of dynasties, any previous treaties and alliances weren't worth the papyrus on which they were inscribed.

> ANY PREVIOUS TREATIES AND ALLIANCES WEREN'T WORTH THE PAPYRUS ON WHICH THEY WERE INSCRIBED.

In the Bible, Sheshonq I is known as Shishak. Not long after Solomon's death, Shishak capitalized on the turmoil Solomon left in his wake. Using a divide-and-conquer strategy, his pillaging forces marched through Israel and then Judah and right into Jerusalem. He "took away the treasures of the house of the LORD and the treasures of the king's house; he took everything. He also took away all the shields of gold that Solomon had made; so King Rehoboam made shields of bronze instead" (1 Kings 14:26, 27, NRSV).

In Solomon's day, everything in the temple was made of gold. But in his son's day, they had to make do with polished brass.

Would you exchange gold for brass—weight for weight?

Of course not, but that's what happened to God's people when they exchanged the wisdom of the Lord for the wisdom of man.

The book of 1 Kings ends with the story of King Ahab's war against Syria. He and Judah's king Jehoshaphat wanted to go recapture some land that the Syrians had taken over. Jehoshaphat insisted on inquiring of the Lord before going into battle, so Ahab brought in four hundred prophets, but none of them spoke for God. Jehoshaphat insisted on hearing from a prophet of God, and Ahab reluctantly agreed.

This is one of the oddest stories in the Bible, but it reveals a couple of important principles:

- There is always more than one kind of prophet abroad in the land. There will always be those who will sell their services—and their message—to the highest bidder. There will always be those who, for the sake of popularity or acclaim, will "prophesy smooth things" and proclaim only positive messages. They aren't to be trusted.
- The majority opinion can be wrong.

But there was one prophet (0.25 percent of those polled) who, at Jehoshaphat's insistence, spoke a true message from the Lord. It wasn't a positive message; it didn't assuage anyone's fears or pander to prickly egos. But it turned out to be right, while the majority message proved wrong. You can read the story, which ended in disaster, in 1 Kings 22.

Ahab didn't want to hear the word of the Lord. He didn't want God's guidance. In fact, when the prophet predicted disaster for him, Ahab had him thrown in jail.

Ahab had power over the man of God.

But God still had power over the man Ahab.

Ahab suffered the consequences of refusing to heed the word of the Lord. He died in battle as a result of his stubbornness and abuse of power. He, like Solomon, fell victim to the perils of power. He exchanged the wisdom of God for the wisdom of man. Gold for brass.

> THIS IS ONE OF THE ODDEST STORIES IN THE BIBLE, BUT IT REVEALS A COUPLE OF IMPORTANT PRINCIPLES.

What about you, friend? Is there gold in your life? Do you seek and find God's will? Or are you satisfied with the mere polished brass of human wisdom?

God offers you His wisdom, His counsel, His way, in His Word, the Bible. Ask Him for it, accept it from Him, then treasure it like gold!

CHAPTER 12

2 Kings: God's History Lesson

Second Kings covers a lot of history. Let me sum it up by telling you the stories of two boys.

The first story is told near the beginning of the book, in chapter 4; the second is found near the end of the book. Because we don't know the first boy's name, I'll call him Elisha's double-miracle boy.

Chapters 4 through 8 tell a series of stories about miracles that Elisha performed, ranging from healing the waters of the spring of Jericho so that it didn't make people sick, to multiplying the oil in a widow's flask so that she had enough to sell and provide a living for her family, and to assisting the kings of Israel and Judah in their war against Moab. Elisha was also the one who told Naaman, the commander of Syria's army, to bathe in the Jordan River in order to be cured of leprosy.

Elisha was quite a traveling man, walking all over the country from Mount Carmel to Jericho to Bethel and back again. Since there were no Hilton Hotels or even Motel 6s along the way, the peripatetic prophet was always glad when someone offered him a place to spend the night.

One family in Shunem even built a new room on the roof of their house exclusively for Elisha when he was in the vicinity.

Shunem was a village on the northern edge of the verdant Jezreel Plain, about fifteen miles from Mount Carmel, the place where

Elisha's predecessor, Elijah, had his showdown with the prophets of Baal.

The Shunamite family had no children and—after many years of marriage—no hope that any would be coming along.

But Elisha asked God for a miracle, and soon the woman of the house had a bouncing baby boy on her knee.

That was miracle number one. Miracle number two came a few years later.

One morning the boy came down with a bad headache. By noon, he had stopped breathing.

His mother knew just what to do. The Jerusalem Bible's translation of the story, which is found in 2 Kings 4, reveals a lot about what life was like for people living in Elisha's day.

After the boy died, the Bible says his mother "went upstairs, laid him on the bed of the man of God, shut the door on him and went out. She called her husband and said, 'Send one of the servants with a donkey. I must hurry to the man of God and back.' 'Why go to him today?' He asked. 'It is not New Moon or sabbath.' But she answered, 'Never mind.' She had the donkey saddled, and said to her servant, 'Lead on, go! Do not draw rein until I give the order.' She set off and came to the man of God at Mount Carmel. . . . When she came to the man of God there on the mountain, she took hold of his feet. . . . She said, 'Did I ask my lord for a son? Did I not say: Do not deceive me?' " (2 Kings 4:21–28).

> WHERE THE WORD OF GOD IS, WHERE THE POWER OF GOD IS, THERE IS LIFE AND THERE IS BLESSING.

Before she said another word, Elisha knew what had happened, and he sent his servant with the staff that Elisha had often used in doing miraculous works, to run ahead and try to raise the child from the dead. Elisha and the woman arrived later and found that the servant had not been able to bring the boy back to life. Elisha himself went up into the room; and in answer to his prayers, God raised the boy back to life, enabling Elisha to give him back to his mother.

What a precious story of God's love and concern for a mother and her little child. But the story teaches more than that. It's a story with an important lesson: where the word of God is, where the power of God is, there is life and there is blessing.

The next story from 2 Kings that we will read happened about two hundred years later, but it makes the same point—with a bit of fine-tuning.

This is the story of Prince Josiah. We first meet him when he's eight years old. His father is the king of Judah, but all is not well in the kingdom.

> THEY RESORTED TO RELIGIOUS AND POLITICAL COMPROMISE—SOMETHING SIMILAR TO WHAT SOLOMON DID WHEN HE MARRIED PHARAOH'S DAUGHTER.

Josiah's father and grandfather were unfaithful kings. Instead of trusting in Judah's God, they built altars to foreign gods—even to the gods of their enemies the Assyrians—right in the Lord's temple in Jerusalem.

Of course, such a betrayal of Judah's God may have been motivated as much by politics as by religion—it may have been the only way they thought they could keep Assyria from attacking them. In other words, they didn't trust the Lord to protect them. Instead, they resorted to religious and political compromise—something similar to what Solomon did when he married Pharaoh's daughter.

Then one day when Prince Josiah was just eight years old, shocking news sped through the streets of Jerusalem.

In this story, it was not the little boy who died, but his father.

King Amon had been assassinated by his servants, right in his own palace!

Chaos reigned in Jerusalem for a time, but when the dust finally settled, the assassins were captured and executed. Then the people of the land took the little boy, Josiah, and put him on his father's throne.

Josiah turned out to be just the opposite of his father and grandfather. He'd no doubt heard stories about his great-grandfather, King Hezekiah, who had been faithful to the Lord and had seen God work miracles in his life many times—even delivering his people from the army of the Assyrians.

So Josiah resolved to be like Great-grandfather Hezekiah. He put his faith in Judah's God, not in political maneuverings or the gods of Assyria.

Second Kings 23:3 reports that Josiah "made a covenant before the LORD, to follow the LORD, keeping his commandments, his decrees, and his statutes, with all his heart and all his soul" (NRSV).

Then he put the words of his covenant into action: "The king commanded the high priest Hilkiah, the priests of the second order, and the guardians of the threshold, to bring out of the temple of the LORD all the vessels made for Baal, for Asherah, and for all the host of heaven; he burned them outside Jerusalem in the fields of the Kidron, and carried their ashes to Bethel. He deposed the idolatrous priests whom the kings of Judah had ordained to make offerings in the high places at the cities of Judah and around Jerusalem; those also who made offerings to Baal, to the sun, the moon, the constellations, and all the host of the heavens" (verses 4, 5, NRSV).

Not content to merely do away with false gods, Josiah led his people in great religious celebrations in honor of the Lord as well—especially the Passover Feast, reminding them of their God and His power to deliver them from bondage to their enemies.

> THE BIBLE DOESN'T OFFER AN UNREALISTICALLY SIMPLIFIED VIEW OF LIFE. IT "TELLS IT LIKE IT IS."

Second Kings 23:25 tells us, "No king before him had turned to the LORD as he did, with all his heart and soul and strength" (NEB). And God rewarded Josiah for his faithfulness. The country prospered under his rule. The people had true freedom for the first time in nearly a century. For thirty wonderful years, none of their old enemies were able to lay a finger on them or oppress them in any way.

And from that you may conclude that the message of 2 Kings is plain and simple: obey God and be blessed; disobey God and suffer. But life is never that simple, and the Bible doesn't offer an unrealistically simplified view of life. It "tells it like it is."

Unfortunately, good King Josiah's life took a tragic twist at the end.

Just four verses after telling us that Josiah served the Lord more faithfully than any other king, 2 Kings reveals what happened in the thirty-first year of his reign: "While Josiah was king, Pharaoh Neco king of Egypt went up to the Euphrates River to help the king of Assyria. King Josiah marched out to meet him in battle, but Neco faced him and killed him at Megiddo" (2 Kings 23:29, NIV).

It was a tragic end to the king's life; and soon after, the kingdom fell to the Egyptians and later, to the Babylonians. It was never free from foreign domination again for more than four hundred years.

Why? Why didn't God continue to protect and bless His faithful king?

Well, it would take a major history lesson to ferret out all the answers. But we can sum it up this way: Josiah's reform—as good as it was—was too little and too late.

Too little, because, by and large, it reformed only the outward behavior of the people. There was no heart change. Even during these seemingly good years, the prophet Jeremiah was heard to complain that

> **Why didn't God continue to protect and bless His faithful king?**

> this people has a stubborn and rebellious heart;
>   they have turned aside and gone away. . . .
> For scoundrels are found among my people;
>   they take over the goods of others.
> Like fowlers they set a trap;
>   they catch human beings.
> Like a cage full of birds,
>   their houses are full of treachery;
> therefore they have become great and rich,
>   they have grown fat and sleek.
> They know no limits in deeds of wickedness;
>   they do not judge with justice
> the cause of the orphan, to make it prosper,
>   and they do not defend the rights of the needy (Jeremiah 5:23, 26–28, NRSV).

Jeremiah sadly assessed what was really going on, even during Josiah's great reform movement. Religion remained superficial. It was something practiced on the Sabbath or on the great feast days. But it didn't change the way people lived on any given Tuesday or Thursday. It didn't change how they treated each other, or how they treated orphans.

The Bible is full of examples of people who were very religious when it came to matters of celebration or observance of rites and sacraments, but whose religion didn't touch their hearts and teach them to love. Jesus' story of the good Samaritan is just one example. He singled out religious leaders as ones who failed to stop and help a man in need. Similarly, the apostle Paul's letters to the Corinthians are addressed to a group of people who were very enthusiastic in their worship, but weren't letting their religion change their morals or their behavior.

God was, and is, always interested in true heart reform, not just enthusiastic worship. In the end, He unfortunately had to allow tragedy to overtake His chosen people to help them learn what was really important.

But out of times of great tragedy came great promise as well. For it was during the times covered in 2 Kings that prophets such as Isaiah and Micah penned their messages that rang down through the centuries with a note of hope for the future.

Isaiah proclaimed, in words familiar to us from Handel's *Messiah:* "Comfort ye, comfort ye my people, saith your God. Speak ye comfortably to Jerusalem, and cry unto her, that her warfare is accomplished, that her iniquity is pardoned: for she hath received of the LORD's hand double for all her sins. The voice of

> OUT OF TIMES OF GREAT TRAGEDY CAME GREAT PROMISE AS WELL.

him that crieth in the wilderness, Prepare ye the way of the LORD, make straight in the desert a highway for our God. Every valley shall be exalted, and every mountain and hill shall be made low: and the crooked shall be made straight, and the rough places plain: And the glory of the LORD shall be revealed, and all flesh shall see it together: for the mouth of the LORD hath spoken it" (Isaiah 40:1–5, KJV).

And the prophet Micah also spoke of the promise of a coming Savior:

> But you, Bethlehem in Ephrathah,
> small as you are to be among Judah's clans,
> out of you shall come forth a governor for Israel,
> one whose roots are far back in the past, in days gone
>   by. . . .
> He shall appear and be their shepherd
> in the strength of the LORD,
> in the majesty of the name of the LORD his God (Micah
>   5:2–4, NEB).

As Josiah's contemporary, Jeremiah, put it: " 'I know the plans I have for you,' declares the Lord, 'plans to prosper you and not to harm you, plans to give you hope and a future' " (Jeremiah 29:11, NIV).

And that is the great lesson we learn from God's history book: He has blessed us in the past, and He has blessings for us in the future as well. Things may not go just as we'd wish every day. Tragedy may stalk our paths, but God's plans for our futures are for good, as we walk with Him in true heart repentance, in true heart religion that changes not just how we worship, but how we live and how we treat others.

Chronicles—Welcome to the Family

When she gave the eulogy for her famous brother, novelist Mona Simpson told of her personal struggle for identity— her childhood dream of someday discovering that she was somebody "special."

Speaking to a packed church, she confessed, "I grew up as an only child, with a single mother. Because we were poor and because I knew my father had emigrated from Syria, I imagined he looked like Omar Sharif. I hoped he would be rich and kind and would come into our lives (and our not yet furnished apartment) and help us."

I suppose that as children we all had dreams of one day discovering that we were actually the son or daughter of a king or wealthy business tycoon.

For most of us, it's only an idle fantasy that eventually fades, as we come to accept that we are ordinary people, with ordinary ancestry, and ordinary lives.

> "ONE DAY A LAWYER CALLED AND SAID HIS CLIENT WAS RICH AND FAMOUS AND WAS MY LONG-LOST BROTHER."

For Mona, it was different, though. She told the crowd gathered to honor the life of her brother about a day in 1985: "By then, I lived in New York, where I was trying to write my first novel. I had a job at a small magazine in an office the size of a closet, with three other aspiring writers. When one day a lawyer called me—me, the middle-class girl from California who hassled the boss to buy us health insurance—and said his client was rich and famous and was my long-lost brother, the young editors went wild. This was 1985 and we worked at a cutting-edge literary maga-zine, but I'd fallen into the plot of a Dick-ens novel and really, we all loved those best. The lawyer refused to tell me my brother's name and my colleagues started a betting pool."*

> THESE BOOKS WERE WRITTEN SPECIFICALLY TO ESTABLISH THE PEOPLE OF ISRAEL IN THEIR UNDERSTANDING OF WHO THEY WERE AND WHERE THEY HAD COME FROM.

It wasn't long, of course, before the mystery was solved. Turns out Mona's long-lost brother was Steve Jobs, cofounder of Apple Computer. And Mona's life would never be the same again, because of her family ties.

Family is important, relationships are important. And when you read the two books of the Bible called Chronicles, you need to understand that some parts of these books were written specifically to establish the people of Israel in their understanding of who they were and where they had come from.

If you find yourself bogging down in the long lists of names, remember that these weren't really written down for you. They were written for people living centuries ago, to help them understand who they were and where they came from.

What kind of person would you be if you couldn't remember anything about your past?

Would I behave differently if I couldn't remember the day I married my dear wife, Debby?

Most of us have known people who've had to go through the heart-wrenching experience of watching a loved one's memories fade.

Did you see the movie *The Notebook* or perhaps read the book? I don't know of anyone who isn't moved to tears by a story like that, of two people very much in love, but only one can remember their life, the joys, the sorrows, the living they shared as husband and wife.

Our past is very important to us—very important to understanding who we are, where we came from, why we are here. And it's also very important as we make decisions about how we're going to live the rest of our lives. So understanding the past is essential to answering life's greatest questions: Who am I? Where did I come from? Why am I here? Where am I going?

And the Old Testament books of 1 and 2 Chronicles were written to help God's people find answers to those questions.

These books were written much later than most of the Old Testament, and they bring that precious commodity called *hindsight* to bear upon the great questions of life.

The books were probably written by the scribe Ezra, or some contemporary of his, sometime after the Jews returned from exile in Babylon. Scholars who read the books in their original language affirm that they probably were written by the same person who wrote the books of Ezra and Nehemiah.

Because Nehemiah carries the story down to about the year 430 B.C., we can assume that's probably about when all four books were written. That means the Chronicles were written long after the books of Samuel and Kings, which cover much of the same history.

> THERE IS A TIME AND PLACE FOR REVIEWING OUR ACTIVITIES TO TRY TO UNDERSTAND WHAT WE DID WRONG THAT GOT US INTO A SITUATION.

Chronicles covers the same territory as these earlier books, but with deeper insights into the story behind the story; that is, more insights into what was going on and *why* events had happened as they did.

You know how, after something bad has happened, people start second-guessing; for instance, going back over the events leading up to the car accident, and saying, "If only I'd gone to the supermarket *before* the cleaners instead of after, this never would have happened."

Second-guessing like that is futile, really, but there is a time and place for reviewing our activities to try to understand what we did wrong that got us into a situation.

An alcoholic waking up on the sidewalk with a splitting headache should probably take some time to review what he or she did wrong that led to the latest binge.

If you have a stomachache, it's a good idea to think back over what you ate at your last meal to see what to avoid eating in the future.

And that, essentially, is what the books of Chronicles do with the history of the people of Judah. They go back over the history of the nation, from the very beginning, and examine what went right and what went wrong and what has brought them to their current situation.

And what is that current situation?

Israel is in dire straits. Their capital city, Jerusalem, has been in ruins for 150 years. The temple has been rebuilt, but the only way they've been able to get anyone to live in the city is to compel one person in ten to leave the farm and move to town.

This abominable situation causes Ezra the scribe to look back over the past and try to figure out what went wrong: the kingdom of Israel—later Judah—started out so well under the leadership of David and Solomon. Why was the nation a failure in Ezra's day?

Ezra gets out the annals, the stories from the past, and he begins to analyze. It's not long before he notices a pattern: when the people have had faith in God and have walked with Him, God has blessed them. But when they have rebelled and turned to other gods, their lives have been filled with disaster after disaster.

Chronicles reads like a litany of lessons from history. The first nine chapters are devoted to establishing Israel's place in the world—there's a genealogical list tracing the royal line all the way from the first man and woman, Adam and Eve, up through David and Solomon and their descen-

> CHRONICLES READS LIKE A LITANY OF LESSONS FROM HISTORY.

dants who sat on the throne of Judah, right up to the time when Babylon came and destroyed Jerusalem. People today tend to skim pretty quickly through the nine chapters of "begats," and rightly so, but in the days when the book was written, these lists were important for establishing a person's birthright and place in the community.

Then there's the story of Saul, Israel's first king—actually just the story of how he died—and an explanation of why things went so badly for him: "So Saul died for his unfaithfulness which he had committed against the LORD, because he did not keep the word of the LORD, and also because he consulted a medium for guidance. But he did not inquire of the LORD" (1 Chronicles 10:13, 14, NKJV).

When the Lord established Israel as a nation, He forbade them from consulting mediums: "The person who turns to mediums and familiar spirits, to prostitute himself with them, I will set My face against that person and cut him off from his people" (Leviticus 20:6, NKJV).

Looking back six hundred years later, Ezra can see the beginnings of a pattern in what happened to Saul. It was when he went against a specific command of the Lord that God abandoned him into the hands of the Philistines.

King David, on the other hand, was a man after God's own heart, and 1 Chronicles 14 tells what happened when the Philistines attacked him. David repeatedly consulted the Lord for guidance, and as verses 16 and 17 report, "David did as God commanded him, and they drove back the army of the Philistines from Gibeon as far as Gezer. Then the fame of David went out into all lands, and the LORD brought the fear of him upon all nations" (NKJV).

SAME ISRAELITE ARMY. SAME ENEMY. SAME BATTLEFIELD. TOTALLY OPPOSITE RESULTS.

Notice the strong contrast between these two stories. Same Israelite army. Same enemy. Same battlefield. Totally opposite results. And what made the difference? Saul consulted a spiritualist medium for counsel, but David consulted the Lord.

After the reign of David's son Solomon, the kingdom of Israel split between the northern tribes, who took the name *Israel,* and the southern tribes, who became the kingdom of Judah. These brother nations often fought with each other, and 2 Chronicles 13:15–18 draws a contrast between the two kingdoms' ways of going about the business of war.

"Then the men of Judah gave a shout; and as the men of Judah shouted, it happened that God struck Jeroboam and all Israel before Abijah and Judah. And the children of Israel fled before Judah, and God delivered them into their hand. . . . Thus the children of Israel were subdued at that time; and the children of Judah prevailed, *because they relied on the LORD God of their fathers*" (2 Chronicles 13:15–18, NKJV; emphasis added).

You don't have to read the entire history of Israel as recorded in the books of Chronicles to get the point. But it does make interesting reading. Over and over again, the same lesson has to be learned. God has called His special people, given them a land to dwell in, and promised them blessings if they'll be faithful to Him. And over and over again, the people have turned to other gods and suffered disasters as a result.

But when the people turned back to God, He was faithful to bless them.

God, you see, had a special purpose in mind for Israel. He established them on the land, at a place that would always be a great crossroads of civilization. He wanted the light of His glory to shine forth in the faces of His people to enlighten the whole world.

Moses reminded his people of this just before they entered the Promised Land, as we read in Deuteronomy 4:5, 6: "Surely I have taught you statutes and judgments, just as the LORD my God commanded me, that you should act according to them in the land which you go to possess. Therefore be careful to observe them; for this is your wisdom and your understanding in the sight of the peoples who will hear all these statutes, and say, 'Surely this great nation is a wise and understanding people' " (NKJV).

> IT'S A LOOK AT WHAT MIGHT HAVE BEEN IF THE PEOPLE HAD REMAINED FAITHFUL.

This was literally fulfilled in the time of Solomon, who Chronicles tells us, "excelled all the kings of the earth in riches and in wisdom. All the kings of the earth sought the presence of Solomon to hear his wisdom, which God had put into his mind" (2 Chronicles 9:22, 23, NRSV).

That's what Chronicles is all about. It's a reminder of the amazing early days of Ezra's people and of the wonderful blessings that God wanted to shower upon them.

It's also a look at what might have been if the people had remained faithful.

Chronicles also looks forward to the future, and Ezra pleads with God's people not to continue to go astray. He reminds them that "Judah was carried away captive to Babylon because of their unfaithfulness" (1 Chronicles 9:1, NKJV).

Ezra, walking the deserted streets of Jerusalem, wants desperately to save his people from being taken into captivity a second time.

We all dream at some time of being connected to great wealth, great power. For Ezra, the dream was a reality. He knew that he and his people were the chosen ones of God—God's own children!

He was like the lawyer who phoned Mona Simpson one day, with news about a long-lost family member. But in this case, the long-lost family member wasn't a business tycoon or prince or earthly king. It was the King of all the universe. And if they would just realize what their heritage was, it would change everything.

Chronicles calls God's people to live as sons and daughters of the King. It calls you and me as well to realize our destiny as sons and daughters of God.

It's good to review our history, our genealogy, and to strive to live in the way that our God would have us to live—in a deep, committed faith relationship with Him. Walking by faith, not sight, not turning aside to the gods of the world.

ENDNOTE

* Mona Simpson, "A Sister's Eulogy for Steve Jobs," Opinion Pages, *New York Times,* October 30, 2011, http://www.nytimes.com/2011/10/30/opinion/mona-simpsons-eulogy -for-steve-jobs.html.

CHAPTER 14

Ezra and Nehemiah: Builders for God

Recently, Focus on the Family reported that, according to their research, born-again Christians are just about as likely to visit a pornography site on the Internet as people who make no claims about their religious beliefs.

What do you think about that? Do you think the church needs a good scourging—a good cleaning up? Do you think we need a bit more hellfire and damnation preaching to straighten people out—perhaps frighten them into better behavior?

Or, do you take a more lenient stance? Do you tend to focus more on the mercy and grace of God and say, "Let's not dwell on people's sins; let's focus on their good points. Let's be like Jesus, who always looked for the best in people"?

THE BOOKS WE'RE STUDYING NOW CONCERN THE LIVES OF TWO MEN WHO HAD VERY LITTLE PATIENCE WITH THE STATUS QUO.

Before I go any further, let me assure you that I believe strongly in the grace of God, and in the ministry of Jesus, who always strove to bring out the best in people. He was the One who selected fishermen, a tax collector, two brothers known as the Sons of Thunder, and even Judas, and worked with them for years, molding and melding their characters, gently turning all but one of them into demonstrations of the power of God's grace.

But the books we're studying now concern the lives of two men who had very little patience with the status quo and insisted on change; they refused to let their nation continue in its complacent faithlessness.

These two men are Ezra and Nehemiah. Each has a book of the Bible named after him.

The book of Ezra begins with the story about the return of the first group of Jewish exiles from the Babylonian captivity. Second Chronicles, the book just before Ezra, ends with the story of how Nebuchadnezzar, king of Babylon, burned down the temple of God in Jerusalem and all the houses and palaces and "took into exile in Babylon those who had escaped from the sword, and they became servants to him and to his sons until the establishment of the kingdom of Persia, to fulfill the word of the LORD by the mouth of Jeremiah" (2 Chronicles 36:20, 21, NRSV).

Chronicles then reports that seventy years later "in the first year of King Cyrus of Persia, in fulfillment of the word of the LORD spoken by Jeremiah, the LORD stirred up the spirit of King Cyrus of Persia so that he sent a herald throughout all his kingdom and also declared in a written edict: 'Thus says King Cyrus of Persia: The LORD, the God of heaven . . . has charged me to build him a house at Jerusalem, which is in Judah. Whoever is among you of all his people, may the LORD his God be with him! Let him go up' " (verses 22, 23, NRSV).

> THIS ERA IS ONE OF THE MOST IMPORTANT TO OUR UNDERSTANDING OF HOW GOD WORKED WITH HIS PEOPLE IN HISTORY.

Ezra picks up the story and tells of the return of a group of exiles in the year 536 B.C., and of the returning exiles' attempts to rebuild the temple in Jerusalem. The story of their twenty-year struggle, and final success, is told in Ezra, chapters 1 through 6. The temple was completed and dedicated in 515 B.C.

Chapter 7 of Ezra jumps ahead to the story of the returned exiles nearly sixty years later in 457 B.C., when the Persian king Artaxerxes sent Ezra and others from Babylon to Jerusalem with orders to make sacrifices to the Lord at the temple in Jerusalem. Artaxerxes not only ordered the offerings and sacrifices to be made but also sent large quantities of silver and gold to buy animals for sacrifice.

Reading straight through the books of Ezra and Nehemiah and

trying to get a clear, chronological picture of how events unfolded can lead to confusion. Ezra sometimes groups events by similarity rather than by sequence.

But this era is one of the most important to our understanding of how God worked with His people in history. It also includes the time of the story of Esther, and coincides with the formative years of Western civilization, when the Greek confederacy of city-states succeeded in twice fending off attacks by the eastern empire of Persia.

Understanding this history is also key to interpreting the prophecies of Daniel 7 and 8.

If you would like to understand this historical era better, the tables I've included in this chapter will help you understand the order of events described in Ezra and Nehemiah. Table 1 lists events in Ezra and Nehemiah in order, with the addition of events in Esther and Haggai and Zechariah. Table 2 lists in chronological order the texts in Ezra that tell the story, skipping the long lists of names.

> WHEN HE HEARD ABOUT THE PEOPLE'S UNFAITHFULNESS, HE LITERALLY TORE OUT HIS HAIR!

Ezra was a scribe, a noted scholar of the Hebrew Scriptures. When he arrived in Jerusalem in 457, he was appalled to find that the returned exiles were not living according to the law of God.

Ezra tells of his reaction to this in chapter 9, verse 3: "When I heard this thing, I tore my garment and my robe, and plucked out some of the hair of my head and beard, and sat down astonished" (NKJV).

When he heard about the people's unfaithfulness, he literally tore out his hair!

Most of us, when we talk about being so frustrated or angry we are "tearing out our hair" are speaking metaphorically. But for Ezra, this was no figure of speech. He literally sat down and tore out some of his hair and beard!

That must have hurt. But he was already in agony of mind because he had discovered that people were letting the ways of the nations around them filter into their lives and take control. They were no longer living for the Lord as they should have.

And that brings us back to the question I asked at the beginning: How do you respond when you hear that Christians are living just like the world around them? Do you respond like Ezra?

A lot of people today might consider Ezra's response extreme. He was so upset that he spent the day weeping and praying before the temple of the Lord, and a large crowd of people gathered around him and began weeping as well.

Under Ezra's tutelage they came to understand that their compromises and intermarriage with heathen peoples was similar to what Israel had done before the Lord allowed them to go into exile; and they came to understand that if they continued to compromise their faith, they could not expect God to bless them.

In a solemn assembly, the people agreed that it was necessary for them to divorce their foreign wives and maintain the purity of their race and their faith.

Much of the book of Ezra focuses on purity and separation from paganism. So it's relevant to our world today, when we see so much of the world creeping into the church.

Some of the things Ezra did—such as forcing men to divorce their foreign wives—seem a bit extreme by today's standards. In order to understand what was going on, it's important to understand that Ezra was dealing with people who were refugees, returning from exile in Babylon. And because he had studied the history of his nation, he believed that a major reason his ancestors had been taken into captivity was that they hadn't remained faithful to God. They had mingled the worship of the Lord with worship of other gods.

Ezra attempted to convince the returning exiles that if they didn't want history to repeat itself, they needed to take seriously the importance of remaining pure in their devotion to the Lord.

Does the world still need people like Ezra, who will fast and pray and kneel in humiliation before the Lord, confessing the disgrace that is in the land because of sin? Does it still need people like those described in Ezra 9:4? "Then everyone who trembled at the words of the God of Israel assembled to me, because of the transgression of those who had been carried away captive" (NKJV).

> THEY NEEDED TO TAKE SERIOUSLY THE IMPORTANCE OF REMAINING PURE.

Do we tremble at the word of the Lord today, or do we just let it float right over our heads without even furrowing our brows?

Could it be that we need a deeper experience with the Lord today as well? Even if it means we have some serious cleaning up to do in our individual lives, or our church's life in order to make it possible for the power of God to work among us in more life-changing ways?

When we see the power of God working, we will see great things happening. That's what happened with Ezra's contemporary, Nehemiah.

Nehemiah came on the scene a few years after Ezra, in about 445 B.C.

When we first meet him, he is living in Shushan, capital of the Persian Empire, and he has an important job as cupbearer to the Persian king, Artaxerxes.

Living in the king's palace, he became privy to a report brought by messengers from Jerusalem, more than 1,200 miles away. Nehemiah was shocked and dismayed when these men reported that the walls of Jerusalem had been broken down and the gates burned with fire. The news brought tears to his eyes. But more than that, it drove him to his knees. Notice how much like Ezra he was. Here's how he described his reaction to the news: "So it was, when I heard these words, that I sat down and wept, and mourned for many days; I was fasting and praying before the God of heaven" (Nehemiah 1:4, NKJV).

> THERE'S MORE TO THE STORY THAN JUST A HABITAT FOR HUMANITY PROJECT.

When King Artaxerxes saw his cupbearer's distress, he sent Nehemiah to Jerusalem, along with a detachment of cavalry and a staff of servants. In fact, he appointed Nehemiah the governor of Judah, with full authority to rebuild the wall and fortify the city.

And Nehemiah went right to work and had tremendous success, because he relied on the Lord and because he was able to rally the people to work with him. But there's more to the story than just a Habitat for Humanity project—great as that was and is.

Three other items come up in the book that peel back the curtain and allow us to see why Nehemiah had such fantastic success.

In chapters 5 and 6, we read two stories that reveal a lot about Nehemiah. The first concerns his attitude toward his opportunity to serve his people. When he arrived in Jerusalem, he discovered that many of the residents had been forced to mortgage their lands, and even sell their children into slavery, just to pay their taxes and debts. Under those circumstances, Nehemiah chose not to use any of the revenues of the land for his own benefit. Instead, he dipped into his own IRA to pay all his expenses, plus the expenses of his staff.

His faithfulness stands out in stark relief against the unfaithfulness of another group of people whom he had to deal with in Jerusalem. Notice this from Nehemiah's prayer found in chapter 6, verse 14: "Remember Tobiah and Sanballat, O my God, because of what they have done; remember also the prophetess Noadiah and the rest of the prophets who have been trying to intimidate me" (NIV).

Tobiah and Sanballat are the bad guys in Nehemiah's story. They're the men who brought their armies up to Jerusalem to try to prevent him from rebuilding the wall around the city. But notice who else was on their side: "the prophetess Noadiah and the rest of the prophets."

> WHEN THE PEOPLE HEARD THE WORDS OF THE LAW, IT MOVED THEM TO TEARS.

Wouldn't you expect the prophets to be on Nehemiah's side when he started rebuilding the city? What's going on here? There's something odd about these prophets who are opposed to rebuilding the holy city.

They were prophets for profit! They had started taking pay from Tobiah and Sanballat, and, because of that, their message was corrupted by money, just like the four hundred prophets Ahab had employed a few centuries earlier.

They no longer spoke for the Lord, but for the highest bidder!

They were just the opposite of Nehemiah, who did the Lord's work for the sheer joy of doing it. And his joy was contagious. When he called the people to the work of rebuilding the wall, they joined him with enthusiasm. But his joy didn't end there.

And that's where the third story comes in. It's found in chapter 8.

It took the people only fifty-two days of enthusiastic labor to close up the wall and secure their city against attack. After they were finished, Ezra began reading the words of God's law to them.

At first, it wasn't a very happy occasion. When the people heard the words of the law, it moved them to tears. They began weeping and mourning, because the law pointed out their sinfulness and failings.

That's what the law is supposed to do. The apostle Paul called it our schoolmaster, to lead us to Christ. To make us aware of our need for God's grace. But the people in Nehemiah's day didn't understand that at first, and they began to weep and moan at the thought of their sinfulness.

But notice how Nehemiah responded: "And Nehemiah . . . said to all the people, 'This day is holy to the LORD your God; do not mourn nor weep. . . . Go your way, eat the fat, drink the sweet, and send portions to those for whom nothing is prepared; for this day is holy to our LORD. Do not sorrow, for the joy of the LORD is your strength' " (Nehemiah 8:9, 10, NKJV).

Did you catch that? Did you notice where Nehemiah found the strength to do all that he did? He didn't find it in the law of God. He didn't do the things he did because he felt guilty.

No, Nehemiah found his strength in the *joy* of the Lord. The strength for all that needed to be done.

How is it with you? Is your strength sometimes lacking? Are you discouraged with life? Do you sometimes think about your sins and feel discouraged? There's nothing wrong with acknowledging your guilt—as both Ezra and Nehemiah did.

But also remember the third lesson of Nehemiah: *Find the joy of the Lord, and let that be your strength.* Learn to serve the Lord with joy and gladness—not out of a sense of guilt, not for profit, or out of fear, but out of the pure *joy* of knowing Him and living in the way He guides you as you study His Word.

TABLE 1

Chronology of Events in the Books of Ezra, Nehemiah, Haggai, Zechariah, and Esther 537–c. 430 B.C.

The books of Ezra and Nehemiah tell the story of the resettlement of Jerusalem between 537 and c. 430 B.C., at the end of the Babylonian exile. The prophets Haggai and Zechariah encouraged the rebuilding of the temple beginning in 520. The story of Esther is also set in this era. This table puts these stories and prophecies in approximate chronological order. The exact dates noted can be determined by reference to astronomy tables that list dates of new moons throughout history. Events recorded in books other than Ezra and Nehemiah are in shaded rows.

	Event	Date (B.C.)	Text
1.	Shortly after conquering Babylon, the Persian king Cyrus issues a decree to rebuild the temple.	September 537	Ezra 1:1–11
2.	Zerubbabel and Jeshua lead 42,360 from Babylon to Jerusalem.	c. 536	Ezra 2:1–70

3.	The returnees rebuild the altar and offer sacrifices.	Sept./Oct. 536	Ezra 3:1–7
4.	In the spring of the following year, the returnees begin construction of the temple.	Apr./May 535	Ezra 3:8–13
5.	Locals offer to help rebuild, but the returnees refuse their offer.	536	Ezra 4:1–3
6.	Locals interfere and stop the rebuilding work until the second year of Darius I.	c. 535–520	Ezra 4:4, 5, 24
7.	Haggai and Zechariah resume rebuilding.	520	Ezra 5:1, 2
7a.	Haggai's first message.	Aug. 29, 520	Hag. 1:1–10
7b.	People respond favorably to Haggai.	Aug. 29	Hag. 1:12
7c.	Haggai's second message, people begin work.	Sept. 21	Hag. 1:13–15
7d.	Haggai's third message.	Oct. 17	Hag. 2:1–9
7e.	Zechariah begins to prophesy.	Oct. or Nov.	Zech. 1:1
7f.	Haggai's fourth and fifth messages.	Dec. 18	Hag. 2:10–19; 20–23
8.	Rebuilding continues and prospers.	520–515	Ezra 6:13, 14
9.	Tattenai and Shethar-Bozenai question rebuilding and write to Darius.	520 or 519	Ezra 5:3–17
10.	Darius finds Cyrus's decree and issues a decree telling Tattenai not to interfere, but rather to support the rebuilding.	519?	Ezra 6:1–12

11. Zechariah has eight visions promising spiritual and temporal prosperity for Judah and Jerusalem and calling God's people to leave Babylon and return to Jerusalem.	Feb. 15, 519	Zech. 1:7–6:15
12. The word of the Lord comes to Zechariah again, promising a glorious future for Jerusalem and destruction of Judah's enemies.	Dec. 7, 518	Zech. 7:1–14:21
13. Reconstruction of the temple is completed.	March 12, 515	Ezra 6:15
14. The temple is dedicated and priests installed.	515	Ezra 6:16–18
15. The returnees celebrate Passover.	Apr. 21, 515	Ezra 6:19–22
16. The only event recorded in Ezra between the completion of the temple in 515 and the year 457 is that the people of the land brought a charge against the inhabitants of Judah at the beginning of Xerxes's reign. In secular history, the Battle of Marathon between the Greeks and Persians occurred in 490.	c. 486	Ezra 4:6
17. Esther replaces Vashti as Xerxes's queen, probably after the Persians were defeated by the Greeks at Plataea in 479.	c. 477	Esther 2:1–18
18. Esther intervenes in a plot against the Jews, sparing them from extermination.	c. 475?	Esther 3:7–9:19

19. Artaxerxes issues a decree allowing Ezra and others to travel to Jerusalem and sacrifice and pray at the temple; the people assemble and begin their journey.	Early 457	Ezra 7; 8
20. Ezra and companions arrive in Jerusalem and rest three days, then present offerings and sacrifices.	July 457	Ezra 7:1–10; 8:32–36
21. Ezra hears of people's unfaithfulness and prays, confessing sins.	Summer/Fall 457	Ezra 9:1–15
22. Shecaniah suggests sending foreign wives away; all the men are called to assemble in Jerusalem.	Dec. 457	Ezra 10:1–8
23. The men assemble in Jerusalem.	Dec. 7, 457	Ezra 10:9–15
24. Those guilty of intermarriage are identified; they send their foreign wives and children away.	Dec. 18, 457–Apr. 15, 456	Ezra 10:16–44
25. Local leaders write to Artaxerxes about the history of rebellion at Jerusalem, and Artaxerxes orders the rebuilding work stopped. (This may have happened in 449 during a revolt by the governor of the area.)	c. 449	Ezra 4:7–23
26. Hanani arrives in Susa and tells Nehemiah that Jerusalem is in ruins; Nehemiah fasts, weeps, prays, confessing the sins of Israel and asking God to grant him mercy.	Dec. 445–Mar. 444	Neh. 1:1–11
27. Nehemiah asks Artaxerxes to send him to Jerusalem.	April 444	Neh. 2:1–8
28. Nehemiah travels to Jerusalem.	Summer 444	Neh. 2:9

29. Local leaders Sanballat and Tobiah are alarmed by Nehemiah's interest in promoting Israel's welfare.	Summer 444	Neh. 2:10
30. Nehemiah rides around the city at night, inspecting the wall.	Summer 444	Neh. 2:11–16
31. Nehemiah galvanizes Jewish leadership; rebuilding begins.	Summer 444	Neh. 2:17, 18
32. Sanballat, Tobiah, and Geshem accuse the Jews of planning to revolt.	Summer 444	Neh. 2:19, 20
33. Teams of Jews begin to repair sections of the wall.	Summer 444	Neh. 3:1–32
34. Sanballat, Tobiah, and others ridicule the work.	Summer 444	Neh. 4:1–3
35. Nehemiah prays for God to judge those opposing the work.	Summer 444	Neh. 4:4, 5
36. When the opponents hear that gaps in the wall have been closed, they plan to attack, causing fear and discouragement.	Summer 444	Neh. 4:6–12
37. Nehemiah encourages the builders and establishes a military guard for those doing the work.	Summer 444	Neh. 4:13–23
38. Nehemiah hears of the plight of the poor and persuades the rich to stop charging usury and confiscating people's fields.	Summer 444	Neh. 5:1–13
39. Nehemiah asks God to bless him because of his faithfulness.	444	Neh. 5:14–19
40. Plotting opponents invite Nehemiah to meet with them. He refuses.	Summer 444	Neh. 6:1–14
41. The wall is finished after only 52 days of work.	Sept. 21, 444	Neh. 6:15, 16

42.	Levites and singers assemble for the dedication of the wall.	444	Neh. 12:27–43
43.	Men are appointed for various roles in the temple service.	444	Neh. 12:44–47
44.	Nehemiah reports that Jewish nobles are allied with Tobiah.	444	Neh. 6:17–19
45.	Gatekeepers, singers, Levites, and local officials are appointed. Security plans are established, but the city is sparsely populated.	Fall 444	Neh. 7:1–5
46.	(List of first settlers.)		Neh. 7:6–73
47.	People assemble at Jerusalem; Ezra reads the law; people weep, then rejoice.	Sept. 26, 444	Neh. 8:1–12
48.	While studying the law, leaders learn about the Festival of Booths; they cut branches, build booths, and live in them for seven days, then hold a solemn assembly on the eighth day.	Sept. 27–Oct. 5, 444	Neh. 8:13–18
49.	In a solemn assembly, the people confess sins, recall God's historical leading and the judgments that resulted from disobedience, appeal for God's help in their current distress. They then sign a pledge to be faithful in the future.	Oct. 19, 444	Neh. 9:1–10:39
50.	Leaders settle in Jerusalem and select by lot one in ten of the rest of the populace to move into the city.	444	Neh. 11:1–36
51.	(List of priests and Levites in Nehemiah's time.)		Neh. 12:1–26
52.	Nehemiah returns to Artaxerxes.	432	Neh. 13:6

53. Eliashib gives Tobiah room in the temple.	After 432	Neh. 13:4
54. In reading the book of Moses, the Jews learn that no Moabites or Ammonites should enter the assembly. They enforce this.	After 432	Neh. 13:1–3
55. Nehemiah returns from Babylon and throws Tobiah out of the temple and has the rooms purified.	After 432	Neh. 13:7–9
56. Nehemiah discovers that the priests and Levites aren't being provided for. He rebukes the officials, gathers Israel, and reinstitutes tithing.	After 432	Neh. 13:10–14
57. Nehemiah enforces Sabbath keeping by closing the city gates before sundown on Friday.	After 432	Neh. 13:15–22
58. Nehemiah chases away those who have intermarried with foreigners.	After 432	Neh. 13:23–28
59. Nehemiah purifies priests, assigns duties, makes provisions for contributions.	After 432	Neh. 13:30, 31

TABLE 2

Reading Ezra in Chronological Order

Text	Date (B.C.)
Ezra 1:1–11 Cyrus tells people to go to Jerusalem; some depart.	Sept. 537
Ezra 2:1, 2, 64–70 Numbers of those who returned and the items they took.	About 536
Ezra 3:1–7 Altar rebuilt in Jerusalem, Feast of Tabernacles observed, offerings begun.	Sept.–Oct. 536
Ezra 3:8–13 Zerubbabel begins overseeing work of building temple; foundation laid.	Apr.–May 535
Ezra 4:1–5 Offer of help from Samaritans turned down; this leads to opposition and stoppage of work for sixteen years.	536–520
Ezra 4:24 Work stopped until 520 B.C.	Up to 520
Ezra 5:17 Haggai and Zechariah encourage rebuilding; Tattenai questions rebuilding, then writes to Darius, telling what the Jews said about Cyrus's decree.	520

Ezra 6:1–12 Darius finds record of Cyrus's decree and orders Tattenai to assist with rebuilding the temple.	519?
Ezra 6:13, 14 Tattenai obeys; Jews finish rebuilding temple.	520–515
Ezra 6:15 Temple finished.	March 12, 515
Ezra 6:16–18 Temple dedicated.	March 515
Ezra 6:19–22 Passover and Feast of Unleavened Bread celebrated.	Apr. 21, 515
Ezra 4:6 Accusation sent to Xerxes.	About 486
Ezra 4:7–23 Accusation sent to Artaxerxes about attempts to rebuild Jerusalem.	Sometime between 465 and 457
Ezra 7:11–27 Ezra receives decree from Cyrus to take people and gold to Jerusalem to offer sacrifices.	Early 457
Ezra 8:21–30 Ezra prepares to go to Jerusalem.	Early 457
Ezra 7:1, 6–10; 8:31 Ezra journeys to Jerusalem.	March–July 457
Ezra 8:32–36 Ezra arrives in Jerusalem and offers sacrifices and delivers the king's orders to government officials.	July 457
Ezra 9:1–15 Report of intermarriage upsets Ezra.	Summer–Fall 457
Ezra 10:1–8 People gather to Ezra and decree that everyone must come to Jerusalem.	Dec. 457

Ezra 10:9–15 Assembly in Jerusalem confesses their sin.	Dec. 7, 457
Ezra 10:16–19; 44 Inquiries into marital status; divorces of pagan wives enforced.	Dec. 18, 457–Apr. 15, 456

CHAPTER 15

Esther: Right Place, Right Time

D id Esther make the right decision? That's one of the questions I'd like to consider as we look at the biblical book named for her.

Her story comes from the heroic era of the Greek and Persian wars—the time of the fateful stand of the three hundred Spartan warriors at the pass of Thermopylae, and Pheidippides's legendary run from Marathon to Athens.

Coming from an heroic era, Esther is a story of a heroine who saved her people from slaughter. But how would she have been regarded if things hadn't turned out so well in the end? Would people have second-guessed and criticized her, condemning her actions?

> HOW WOULD SHE HAVE BEEN REGARDED IF THINGS HADN'T TURNED OUT SO WELL IN THE END?

Esther was born in Persia not long before the famous battle of Marathon, which pitted the Greeks against an invading Persian army in 490 B.C. Her story involves the Persian emperor Xerxes, son of Darius the Great, the emperor who was defeated at Marathon. After his father's death, it fell to King Xerxes to try to avenge the Persian defeat.

In 481 B.C., Xerxes marched toward Athens with the largest army ever assembled in the ancient world. Because many of his father's ships had been wrecked near Mount Athos, his engineers dug a mile-long canal through a peninsula to guarantee his navy safe passage. His army marched across the mile-wide Hellespont on a pontoon bridge made up of ships' hulls strung together with papyrus cables—an engineering feat unrivaled in ancient military history.

After overcoming the three-hundred-man Spartan blockade at Thermopylae, Xerxes's army marched on Athens and burned the temples on the Acropolis. But a few days later, his navy was destroyed in the Battle of Salamis, and Xerxes turned tail and headed back to Persia.

This Persian king who plays a role in the story of Esther was no small player on the world stage. In the Bible, he is called Ahasuerus, only because of some confusion that was introduced many years ago when Xerxes's name was transliterated to Babylonian, then to Latin.

Back in Persia, he had another conquest to concentrate on, taking his mind off the embarrassment of defeat on the battlefield.

Prior to leaving for Greece, he had banished his queen, Vashti, for disobeying his command. Now he turned his attention to finding a new queen. And that's where Esther comes into the story.

I'm sure you've heard her story before. But before you finish this chapter, why not get out your Bible and read it again to refresh your memory? It takes less than half an hour to read.

> SHE WAS NAMED FOR THAT BEAUTIFUL TREE WITH STAR-SHAPED FLOWERS THAT GROWS ABUNDANTLY IN ISRAEL, HER HOMELAND.

I want to look at this story and ask some questions about it that you may have thought about before, but put out of mind. They're questions that aren't raised in your typical Bible storybook for children, but which naturally come to mind when you read the story as an adult.

Hadassah (her Jewish name) was being raised by her cousin Mordecai in Susa, one of the capital cities of the Persian Empire, in the fifth century B.C. Now, put yourself in the place of this young woman. Hadassah's name means "Myrtle." She was named for that beautiful tree with star-shaped flowers that grows abundantly in Israel, her homeland.

The myrtle was one of the trees that the Jews would use to build shelters when they celebrated the Feast of Tabernacles—the festival that reminded them of the Exodus and how God had redeemed them from captivity in Egypt.

Hadassah's very name reminded the Jewish people who were captives in the Persian Empire that they shouldn't be living in captivity. They should be living in freedom in their own homeland, Israel. In fact, some Jews already had gone back to the Promised Land fifty years before when the Persian Empire overthrew the Babylonians. Apparently, Hadassah's grandparents had chosen to stay in Persia instead, but perhaps her parents named their first daughter Myrtle as a sort of promise to themselves that one day they would take their family home to the Promised Land.

SHE WAS OFFERED THE OPPORTUNITY TO BE A CONTESTANT ON THE LATEST REALITY TV SHOW, *WHO WANTS TO MARRY A KING?*

But Hadassah's parents died when she was young, and her cousin Mordecai took her in. Then, when she was still a young girl, she was offered what seemed to be the opportunity of a lifetime—but was it really?

Basically, she was offered the opportunity to be a contestant on the latest reality TV show, *Who Wants to Marry a King?*

Because the king needed a replacement queen, Esther 2:3, 4 tells us that his counselors suggested that he "appoint commissioners in all the provinces of his kingdom to gather all the beautiful young virgins to the harem in the citadel of Susa. . . . And let the girl who pleases the king be queen instead of Vashti" (NRSV).

The king liked this idea, so messengers were sent all through the huge Persian Empire, looking for the most beautiful young virgins to "invite" them to try out for the "show."

Now, I use the word *invite* advisedly. It wasn't easy to turn down an invitation to an audience with the king. Shaking one's head the wrong way in response to a king's invitation usually led to the removal of one's head! Even a queen was not allowed to say No to the king. Vashti's experience had proven that.

So, put yourself in Hadassah's shoes.

How would you have responded to the invitation?

And while you're pondering that question, let me throw just a little more grist into the mill.

Let's fit this story into the context of Jewish history. It takes place just a few years before the time of Ezra and Nehemiah.

Do you remember what upset Ezra so badly when he returned to Jerusalem? Remember, he was so distraught when he heard about it that he sat down in the city square, ripped his clothes to shreds, and literally tore out some of his hair.

What made Ezra tear out his hair? He heard that young Jewish men and women were marrying foreigners. And that was leading to impurity, idolatry, and unfaithfulness to God.

There was strong sentiment against intermarriage with foreigners among Jews who were faithful to God.

But what if the foreigner who was looking for a wife was the most powerful king on the planet? Would that make a difference?

What if you, as a young Jewish girl, were "invited" to play that game, *Who Wants to Marry a King?* Would you accept the invitation?

Now, imagine you're Hadassah. Your cousin Mordecai says, "Hey, if you've been invited to try out for queen of the empire, go for it! Just don't tell them your name is Hadassah—they'll know you're a Jew. Tell them your name is . . . Ishtar. That's the name of the goddess the Babylonians call the queen of heaven. It's a great name for a queen."

Wait a minute—you might be saying—I thought we were talking about Queen Esther, not Queen Ishtar.

Well, the fact is that we call her Esther, but the Persians no doubt called her Ishtar—the name of the most important goddess in the Babylonian pantheon.

> THERE WAS STRONG SENTIMENT AGAINST INTERMARRIAGE WITH FOREIGNERS AMONG JEWS WHO WERE FAITHFUL TO GOD.

So now how do you respond, if you're Hadassah? Not only are you being told to try out for the right to marry a foreigner, you're being told to take the name of a heathen goddess.

That casts a different light on the story of Esther with which some people might not feel comfortable. This isn't the way you read the story in most Bible storybooks. But when I read the Bible, I like to probe deeply into the Book of books. When you do that, you often find the grace and goodness of God revealed in new ways. Follow me on this—I think you'll see what I mean.

As the story is told in the book of Esther, Hadassah doesn't seem to have had any qualms about trying out for the position of queen.

"When the king's order and edict had been proclaimed, many girls were brought to the citadel of Susa and put under the care of Hegai. Esther also was taken to the king's palace and entrusted to Hegai, who had charge of the harem. The girl pleased him and won his favor. Immediately he provided her with her beauty treatments and special food. He assigned to her seven maids selected from the king's palace and moved her and her maids into the best place in the harem. Esther had not revealed her nationality and family background, because Mordecai had forbidden her to do so" (Esther 2:8–10, NIV).

Now, I've read books that made it sound like Esther merely entered some sort of beauty pageant or sweepstakes contest to see who would be queen. But that's not the way the Bible reads. Here's what would happen to a young woman after she'd been thoroughly prepared for her encounter with the king: "This is how she would go to the king: Anything she wanted was given her to take with her from the harem to the king's palace. In the evening she would go there and in the morning re-

> ESTHER WENT INTO THE KING'S CHAMBERS A VIRGIN—AND CAME OUT A CONCUBINE!

turn to another part of the harem to the care of Shaashgaz, the king's eunuch who was in charge of the *concubines*. She would not return to the king unless he was pleased with her and summoned her by name" (Esther 2:13, 14, NIV; emphasis added).

Whoa. That's heavy. Esther went into the king's chambers a virgin—and came out a concubine!

She went in pure—and came out compromised.

Now, why am I pointing this out? Am I trying to shock you—or spoil what you thought was the story of a courageous, honorable woman?

No. Not at all. I'm telling you this because I know that there may be someone reading this who feels like a thoroughly compromised man or woman. Someone who's made all kinds of wrong choices. You've wandered away from God. You haven't stood up for what you knew was right. And now you find yourself in trouble. Maybe you feel as if God has abandoned you—that you've gone too far down the wrong road to turn back. Or maybe you know someone else who feels this way.

Listen: Esther is the story of a woman who—if we wanted to hold up the highest biblical standards against her life—we could find all kinds of ways to find fault with her. There are no doubt plenty of people who would shake their fingers at her, shame her, and remind her of all the "wrong" choices she had made.

Let's face it: her decisions would have gotten her disfellowshiped from many churches!

But God didn't abandon her. In fact, when she chose to take her stand with God's people, God was right there for her and made her into a heroine for His cause.

God apparently blessed her in her time with the king, because Esther 2:17 tells us that "the king loved Esther . . . ; of all the virgins she won his favor and devotion, so that he set the royal crown on her head" (NRSV).

It wasn't long after this that Esther's nation—the Jews—came under serious threat of being wiped out in a Persian fit of ethnic cleansing, and Esther's cousin challenged her with the famous question: "Who knows but that you have come to royal position for such a time as this?" (Esther 4:14, NIV).

> HER DECISIONS WOULD HAVE GOTTEN HER DISFELLOWSHIPED FROM MANY CHURCHES!

Because of the position she was in, Esther was able to avert this disaster.

Even though she had made some decisions that may have set people's tongues wagging.

Even though she took a path in life that could have gotten her kicked out of the church.

Still, when she was willing to make herself available to do the will of God, God was able to use her.

And that gives me so much courage. That gives me so much joy!

Because I know I've made mistakes.

I know people could—and probably do—gossip about some of my failings.

But still, I want to make myself available to God, to do what He calls me to do.

How about you?

Would you like to be a hero or heroine for God? It's not too late. You're not too far down the wrong road. You can still turn to God, just as Esther did. And do you know what? He'll not only make you a hero or a heroine. He'll make you a king or a queen—for all eternity. To reign with Him. That's what God's grace is all about.

God chose Esther to do great things. And even though Esther chose some paths in life that might not have seemed right at the time, God didn't abandon her. When she gave herself to Him, He used her in marvelous ways.

He's chosen you for great things, too, now and in eternity. Whoever you are. Wherever you are. He's chosen you.

Job: The Story of Jim

The book of Job appears to be an ancient drama, with speaking parts for various participants, including a narrator, God, Satan, Job, and a number of Job's friends.

In 2001, when our Voice of Prophecy team was discussing how best to bring this old, well-known story to life for twenty-first-century listeners, we hit upon the idea of re-creating the drama in a modern setting.

Here's how we retold the story, using events current to that year—including power shortages and the collapse of the Internet stock bubble—to help listeners be better able to relate to the characters in one of the most famous dramas in the world.

In case you want to read the ancient story and the modern one together, I've occasionally inserted chapter markers in this version.

The Story of Jim

NARRATOR:

I'd like to tell you a story about a man named Jim. He lived in Palm Desert, California. He had a huge house there—right beside a golf course. He lived there only during the winter months. Summers found him in his cliffside house in Malibu, or sometimes at his manor outside Sydney, Australia. He was a good man. All his money had been made in honest ways—he had nothing to do with underhanded dealings.

He had a wife, seven sons, and three daughters. His portfolio included controlling interests in some of the fastest-rising Internet enterprises and thousands of shares of stock in the two largest power utilities in California. He had limousines and chauffeurs in every city where his companies had offices.

He'd done everything he could to raise his kids right, but you know how the children of the wealthy are. His sons felt as if life had been handed to them on a silver platter. They spent a lot of their time throwing big parties for each other, and, of course, they invited their sisters too. Jim was concerned about them. He worried that they might be offending God, so after their parties he'd always go to church and say prayers for them, asking God to forgive anything they might have said or done wrong.

Now, while all this was going on, God and Satan got into a conversation.

GOD:

"You know, Satan, you think you're king of the earth, and that you have everyone in your power. But have you noticed Jim? He's blameless, totally against your unrighteous ways."

SATAN:

"Sure I've seen him, but it's obvious why he's so good. You've blessed his stock portfolio and protected his house and his kids. You're a veritable Santa Claus to the guy. Just take all that away from him, and see if he's still Your friend!"

> "IT'S OBVIOUS WHY HE'S SO GOOD. YOU'VE BLESSED HIS STOCK PORTFOLIO AND PROTECTED HIS HOUSE AND HIS KIDS."

GOD:

"All right. Everything he has is in your hands. But don't you dare harm him physically."

NARRATOR:

A few days later, Jim's sons and daughters were off in Oklahoma, partying at the oldest son's house, when corporate raiders bought out several of Jim's companies and used their capital to dissolve the debts of their own failed companies, leaving Jim with nothing but worthless stock. Then an energy crisis hit California, and Jim's stock in the power companies began to plummet as talks of bankruptcy sent Wall Street traders scurrying for cover. Jim ended up having to hand out pink slips to some of his most trusted employees. When news of his financial problems spread, a repossession company took away all his limousines at the stroke of midnight one night, and the next day they came after his helicopters and private jets.

> A REPOSSESSION COMPANY TOOK AWAY ALL HIS LIMOUSINES AT THE STROKE OF MIDNIGHT.

But the worst blow came when CNN reported that an F5 tornado had ripped through Oklahoma, smashing Jim's oldest son's house and killing all ten of his children.

All along Jim had been saying,

JIM:

"It can't get any worse than this."

NARRATOR:

But now he knew it could get worse. Haggard, worn, exhausted, and feeling dead inside, Jim ripped his Armani suit to shreds and shaved off all his hair. He stumbled out into the backyard of his Palm Desert home, looking up at the sky, then fell to his knees and finally flat on his face, sobbing uncontrollably.

When the first wave of sorrow had passed, he looked up and spoke—mainly to himself.

JIM:

"I guess I came into the world with nothing, and I will leave with nothing. God is good. He gives; He takes away. But He's still good and blessed."

NARRATOR:

In spite of his sorrow, Jim wouldn't say anything against God.

The next time Satan was allowed into God's presence, they talked about Jim again.

GOD:

"Didn't I tell you Jim would remain faithful even though I let you wreck his life?"

SATAN:

"You didn't let me touch him, though. Those humans have a saying, 'As long as you have your health . . .' you know. Let me touch his body with sickness—then see how nice he talks to You."

GOD:

"All right, you can do whatever you like to him, short of killing him."

NARRATOR:

So Satan made Jim so sick—boils all over his body. The poor guy was miserable, sitting out on a sand pile in an undeveloped area behind his house. His wife walked out into the backyard, took one look at him, and said,

MRS. JIM:

"You'd be better off dead. Why don't you just curse God and die?"

JIM:

"Don't be silly. If you can take good from God, can't you accept bad from Him as well?"

> "IF YOU CAN TAKE GOOD FROM GOD, CAN'T YOU ACCEPT BAD FROM HIM AS WELL?"

NARRATOR:

Just then, three of Jim's friends drove up in their golf carts: Elwin, the pastor of Jim's church; Bruce, the head elder; and Frank, the chairman of the visitation committee. They had come over to cheer him up a bit, but the sight of him stole the breath right out of their lungs. He was a lot worse off than they could have imagined. They got out of their carts and just sat down beside him, utterly speechless.

They sat there in silence for a long time.

Chapter 3

When Jim finally spoke, it was to curse the day he'd been born:

JIM:

"You know what? I wish I'd never been born. I wish my parents had never sent out birth announcements. I'd rather have been still-born than be the way you see me today. At least then I'd be resting quietly in my grave. Even wicked people find rest in death.

"Tell me, Pastor, if you can. Why should people be born if it's just for suffering? They spend their lives wishing they were dead. A guy spends his life trying to eat right, working out at the gym, trying to do everything right, but ends up like this anyhow!"

PASTOR ELWIN:

"Jim, I'm almost afraid to answer. What can I say?

"Remember, Jim, how you used to encourage other people who had problems. But now—now that the shoe's on the other foot, all you can do is complain! Where's your faith?

> "THESE KINDS OF THINGS JUST DO *NOT* HAPPEN TO THE GOOD. GOD PUNISHES THE WICKED, NOT THE RIGHTEOUS."

"Listen . . . how can I put this gently? You've been a good man—but these kinds of things just do *not* happen to the good. God punishes the wicked, not the righteous. This word came to me by direct revelation from God. You know how righteous He is. Even angels can't measure up—so how could you or anyone else really be blameless in His sight?

"Look around you—it's the fools and sinners who get knocked down and lose their shirts on the stock market. It doesn't just come out of the blue—it's the result of their sins.

"If I were you, here's what I would do: I'd get down on my knees and pray. Plead your cause with God. He's merciful. He forgives and restores people. In a way, you should actually be happy these horrible things have happened to you—to call you up short and keep you from becoming more wicked. Repent, Jim! God will restore your fortunes. I'm sure of it."

JIM:

"Excuse me, but I think I have a right to be upset! My problems are absolutely overwhelming. God Himself has attacked me. I'm so sick I can't even enjoy my food anymore.

"If I could ask God for one thing, it would be to kill me! How strong does He think I am to have to endure this kind of suffering?

"You know what? I'd have expected something better from you, Pastor. You ought to be here to comfort me, but you're about as useful as a broken drinking fountain on a golf course. A guy could die of thirst on the third hole if he had to rely on you for comfort. But have I ever even asked you for help of any kind?

"Look, if you can point out what I've done wrong, I'll listen. But you're on my case for no reason at all. What do you know about anything—look at me? Do you think I'm lying to you? Do you question my integrity?

"Everyone suffers, but I suffer more than most people. I toss and turn all night, I suffer all day long with boils. The good days are all gone for me—the only thing I have to look forward to is death.

"I wish I could die. But I won't go out with a whimper. I've got to have answers from God. Why is He punishing me like this?"

Chapter 8

NARRATOR:

Bruce, the church head elder spoke up:

BRUCE:

"Jim, I'm gonna give it to you straight. You're rambling on like a long-winded old coot. Face it. Your sons and daughters were sinners; that's why God killed them. Now, wake up. You need to seek God for yourself. If you do, He'll forgive you for whatever He's punishing you for and bless you again.

"Ask around—ask the old folks who've been around for a long time. They'll tell you. Putting greens don't sprout up in the desert without water. Shut off the sprinklers, and the golf course dries up. That's what happens with good men who go bad too. They wither and die. God uproots them. But there's still time to repent, Jim! Turn back to God, and He'll raise you up again. You'll get the best of the guys who are laughing behind your back yet!"

"TURN BACK TO GOD, AND HE'LL RAISE YOU UP AGAIN."

Jim:

"So, that's what you think of me. Well, you want to know what I think? I think I haven't got a snowball's chance in Waikiki. God is so much bigger than me; how can I argue with Him? Who can resist Him and survive? He made the whole universe. Even if I am right, how can I persuade Him of it? Even if I could call Him into court, I doubt He'd listen. He's been downright cruel to me for no reason—no reason at all!

> "I TRY TO CHEER UP AND 'JUST KEEP SMILING'—BUT THINGS ONLY GET WORSE."

"I can proclaim my innocence all I want—but what good will it do me?

"You know what—it doesn't make any difference to God. When disaster strikes, it hits the good and the bad together.

"I try to cheer up and 'just keep smiling'—but things only get worse. God is so far above me. I wish there was a mediator—someone to get Him to lay off me so I could speak to Him. I know I haven't done anything to deserve this!

"I am sick of it!

"I'm just gonna let it all hang out!

(Shouting toward the sky.) "God! Stop condemning me! Tell me why You're letting all this happen to me! Are you getting some sort of jollies out of making me suffer? If You were mortal like me, You'd have compassion instead of picking through my life looking for some little sin to punish me for!

"You're the One who made me! Was it just so You could find fault in me and punish me?

"Why did You even give me life in the first place? Why didn't You let me be stillborn? Life's short. Just go away and *leave me alone* so I can be happy for a few minutes before I die and go into oblivion."

Narrator:

Frank, the chairman of the church visitation committee, spoke up next.

Frank:

"Jim, you've always been pretty good with words. But such a speech demands a response. You ramble on so much—are you afraid to hear what we have to say?

"You think you're always right. You proclaim, 'I'm guiltless before God.'

"But what if God could get a word in edgewise? He'd have something to say to you—He's a lot wiser than you are, and He hasn't punished you as badly as your sins deserve!

"God is so far beyond you—you haven't got a clue about Him! But He knows all about you— your hypocrisy, your shady deals.

"Look at you! You're such a fool no one can teach you anything! You ought to be

> "IT'S EASY TO LOOK DOWN YOUR NOSE AT THE UNFORTUNATE WHEN YOU'RE RIDING AROUND IN A LIMO."

praying, not criticizing God! You ought to be repenting, not moaning. Do that, and things will get better. But if you try to ignore or hide your sin, you haven't got a prayer!"

Chapter 12

JIM:

"Well, aren't you guys the fount of all wisdom!

"Listen, I'm just as good as you, but you make me a laughingstock in spite of my innocence.

"I'll tell you what. It's easy to look down your nose at the unfortunate when you're riding around in a limo. But a lot of wicked people are doing just fine.

"God is in control of everything. He raises men up and puts them down. He can make the wise foolish. I know all this, but what I want is a chance to talk to God and argue my case.

"I wish you guys would just shut up and let your silence be your wisdom. You're not speaking for God. Does He need you to speak for Him? And, by the way, how well do you think you'd come off if He questioned you? Not so good, I'll bet.

"Just be quiet and let me speak—I'll stick my neck in the noose—I can't be silent even for fear of God's wrath. If I can just get my day in court, I know I'll be acquitted.

"God, here's all I want: take Your hand off me and let me speak without fear. What am I being punished for? Why do You treat me like an enemy and enslave me? I'm just a short-lived man. Why should

You pick on someone so small and insignificant? Just leave me alone!

"Even trees are better off than human beings—if You cut them down, they'll sprout up again, but when we die, that's it for us. I could take it if the grave was just a temporary resting place and I knew You'd remember me and call for me again. But right now You're just picking on me for anything I ever did wrong, and I've about had it. I'm about to collapse in despair."

PASTOR ELWIN:

"If you had a nitwit's sense, you wouldn't be spouting worthless words like that, Jim! Have you no fear of God? You think you ought to be invited to speak directly to Him, do you? I didn't realize how low you'd gone. Your own words condemn you!

"Who do you think you are, anyhow? Do you have half a clue what's going on in God's heavenly counsel? What makes you so much smarter than us? We have the old, wise people on our side. Why are you so bold as to vent at God? You ought to realize that it's impossible to be blameless before Him.

"If you'll be quiet long enough to listen, I'll share the wisdom of the ages with you: It is the wicked man who is fearful and who is struck down suddenly as you have been. No matter how prosperous he's been, he'll lose it all. He thinks he's above all that, but everything he has comes to naught. Godless people are the ones who suffer a fate like yours, Jim. Godless people, not the righteous!"

> "IN ALL MY SUFFERING, I REMAINED SINCERE. ONE IN HEAVEN PLEADS MY CAUSE."

JIM:

"You think you're telling me something new, Pastor? And you, Bruce? And you, Frank? You're just making things worse, not better.

"Look, trade places with me for fifteen minutes, and then see how you like it if I harangue you. I wouldn't do that to you. I'd try to cheer you up.

"But as it is right now, it makes no difference whether I speak or keep silent. I still suffer. Then you guys come along and rub salt in my wounds! God has left me at the mercy of people like you. I was just fine till He attacked me, shooting His arrows right through me.

"In all my suffering, I remained sincere. One in heaven pleads my cause. I just wish there was someone to arbitrate for me—I don't have much longer to live. Men taunt me—God, help me! The innocent are puzzled, wondering, What's the point of righteousness if this happens to me? But still they stick to the course.

"Come on, you guys. Try again. Speak up. Show me some wisdom this time. My life is like a fading echo—I can't take any of my good deeds down to the grave with me."

Chapter 18

BRUCE:

"Like a fading echo, are you? You *ought* to be silent. Take some time to think this thing through; then we'll talk. Why do you treat us like dumb cows? Is there anything you wouldn't do to prove yourself innocent?

> "I KNOW I HAVE A VINDICATOR. IN THE END HE'LL SPEAK FOR ME IN COURT."

"Listen, we all know that it's the wicked man who suffers in darkness and dies. He's paralyzed with fear; his skin rots away. His house is full of pill bottles and miracle potions, but he wastes away and dies childless anyway. That's the fate of evildoers like you, Jim, and those who care nothing for God."

JIM:

"How long are you guys gonna keep this up? This attacking me, insulting me. If I did wrong, it's me who's wrong, but you're gloating—telling me I'm just getting what I deserve.

"All I can say is, Yes, it is God who has done this to me. He has ensnared me, stripped me, beaten me down. He treats me like an enemy. Everyone ignores me and treats me like an alien. Even my butler won't listen to me. My wife can't stand to be around me because my breath stinks. Those I love the most avoid me.

"Take pity on me, if you're my friends. The hand of God has struck me—must you do so too? You're like a bunch of cannibals devouring my flesh!

"I wish my words could be written in stone to witness to me.

"But you know what? Despite all this, I know I have a Vindicator. In the end, He'll speak for me in court. God Himself will vindicate me, and I'll see Him with my own eyes!

"I feel depressed—suicidal—listening to you guys tell me I've brought all this on myself. So, beware. Condemnation is a two-edged sword, and one day soon it's liable to be pointing at you! Then you'll know what it is to be under judgment!"

FRANK:

"I can't sit here quietly any longer and listen to these stupid arguments, Jim. The Holy Spirit is giving me answers for you: Don't you realize that a wicked man prospers only briefly—just like you did—and then he'll be swept away? No matter how high and mighty he becomes, it will all come to naught and his family ends up poverty-stricken. His wickedness tastes good at the time; but in the end, it will make him vomit! He becomes greedy, eating everything, but then God strikes him, piercing him with arrows (as you say God has done to you). He's enveloped in darkness; his house is swept away.

"Jim, all I'm saying is, if the shoe fits, wear it."

JIM:

"I wish you guys would just listen to me—that would be enough comfort. Listen for a minute; then you can mock me all you want. Don't I have a right to express my thoughts too? Look at my plight and put your hand over your mouth. I'm utterly horrified at my condition.

> "DO YOU REALLY THINK IT'S ANY BENEFIT TO GOD IF YOU'RE AS RIGHTEOUS AS YOU SAY YOU ARE?"

"Here's what I'd like to know: Why do wicked people have long, prosperous lives with no calamities? They tell God to leave them alone, and He does. He lets them die in peace after a long life of wickedness.

"How often, really, do you see the wicked get what's coming to them? How often does God give them what they deserves?

"I know what you'll say—'Well, the trouble they earned will come to their sons'—but what justice is there in that? Why don't they reap their own just desserts? It seems to me like there's no rhyme or reason to who prospers and who doesn't—everyone dies in the end anyhow, some in health, some in illness.

"I know what you're thinking. You're going to ask me, 'Where is the great man's house now—didn't he reap what he sowed?' But you guys are entirely too parochial. You ought to ask people who've traveled a bit. They'll tell you that there are many places in the world where the wicked are spared all disaster and are even given big, honorable funerals."

Chapter 22

PASTOR ELWIN:

"Jim, do you really think it's any benefit to God if you're as righteous as you say you are? Do you think He's done all this to you because you're so pious?

"Jim, I have to say this to you, as your pastor. God has done this to you because you are so wicked. You've turned your back on the poor, the thirsty, the homeless, the widows. You've acted like God wasn't watching anything you did.

"Think about it. Wicked men die young because they basically tell God to bug off and leave them alone, even though He filled their homes with good things. Their money evaporates, and the righteous have the last laugh.

"Jim, what you need is simple. One word: Surrender. Give yourself to God. Stop rebelling. If you'll repent and stop trusting in your riches, God will be your gold and silver. Learn to *really* trust God; then you'll be able to face Him. Pray to Him, and He will bless you. God brings down the pride of the haughty, but if you're innocent, He'll save you!"

> "GOD HAS A DAY OF RECKONING, WHEN THE WICKED WILL GET WHAT THEY HAVE COMING TO THEM."

JIM:

"I am totally fed up with this! God has really been rough on me. I just wish I knew where to find Him so I could plead my case before Him and find out what He has to say. Do you think He would browbeat me like you guys have been doing?

"I don't think so! He wouldn't file any charges against me. He would vindicate me.

"But I've looked everywhere for Him and can't find Him. I've done everything He instructed, but He's the One who decides the fate of man. That makes me fearful of Him, but it still won't make me be silent before Him.

"God has a day of reckoning, when the wicked will get what they have coming to them for taking advantage of the downtrodden. There are a lot of poor people who suffer horribly at the hands of the wicked, and God doesn't answer their prayers. There are people who lay all kinds of evil plans and carry them out in the darkness—murder, adultery, thievery. God may let them prosper for a while; but in the end, God will snap them like a stick. (I know that, but still I don't fear His judgment.) If I'm wrong in my understanding, show me where."

> "THE FEAR OF THE LORD IS WISDOM, AND TURNING AWAY FROM EVIL IS UNDERSTANDING."

BRUCE:

"You know what, Jim? Even the moon and stars aren't perfect in God's sight, so how do you think you're so pure before Him? None of us are anything more than maggots and worms to Him!"

JIM:

"Do you guys really think you've helped me somehow? What have you done to help a man who's at his wits' end? God is the One who's all-powerful.

"But you know what, despite all that's happened to me, still I won't lie or admit to anything you've accused me of. I am innocent. I hope my enemies reap the fate of the wicked who are cut off by God despite their riches. But God's wisdom is far too deep—no one can find it no matter how deep they dig for it. All we can do is seek it and righteousness, for the fear of the Lord is wisdom, and turning away from evil is understanding.

"You've heard that song, haven't you—'Yesterday, all my troubles seemed so far away . . . oh, I believe in yesterday'? I wish I could go back to the time when God was taking care of me. People respected me; they listened to me then and spoke well of me. I helped so many people, protecting them from the shysters that would have preyed on them.

"But now look at me. Bums I wouldn't have hired to clean my barn laugh at me. God no longer hears my cry for help. He's going to let me die helpless, even though I never turned my back on anyone who cried out to me.

"I expected good in return for what I'd done, but look what it got me. Isn't it the wicked that God is supposed to send trouble upon? What about me? I've tried so hard to do good. I never lusted after women, never wandered in evil. I've been kind to others. I'll take my punishment like a man—for whatever I've done wrong. But I haven't turned to other gods or failed to pay my debts. I've never repaid evil for evil or been inhospitable or deceitful. If there's a case to be made against me, let me see it. I'll let the whole world know of my evil deeds.

"But my life is my witness. I'll go to court any day and stand trial for what I've done. That's all I have to say."

Chapter 32

NARRATOR:

The pastor and his associates finally gave up trying to talk to Jim, because they couldn't convince him of his sinfulness. Jim's young golf caddy, Eddy, had happened along about the time the other three men arrived, and he'd sat quietly, listening, hoping to glean some wisdom from the older men's speeches. By now he was getting angry—first with Jim for claiming to be more righteous than God, but also with the three friends who hadn't been able to answer Jim and had let God be made to look bad. Finally he spoke up:

> "IF YOU'LL JUST ADMIT YOUR SIN AND REPENT, GOD WILL HELP YOU."

EDDY:

"You know, I'm just a young guy. I didn't think I should speak up in such august company, but you know what—I've figured out that age doesn't bring wisdom. You guys have gotten absolutely nowhere with Jim.

"Come on, Jim, listen to me. I feel sure I'm right about this: God made me just like He made you. But it's you who's ended up on a bed of pain. God does things like this to men to correct them.

"If there's even one angel in heaven who's pleading your case and telling God how good a man you are, you'll start getting better. Or, if you'll just admit your sin and repent, God will help you. Listen to me, Jim. If you have something to say, say it, otherwise, listen.

"Listen carefully while I formulate my argument. Think about this: what is really right? Jim says he's innocent, that God has dealt unjustly with him.

"How irreverent! How despicable! To say that doing good doesn't bring good! That's casting aspersions on God Himself. God isn't evil. He doesn't play false. He pays people back for what they do. If He pulls the plug on us, we're all about as useful as burned-out lightbulbs.

> "GOD DOES NOT LET THE WICKED PROSPER. HE HELPS THE POOR AND SUFFERING."

"Think about it, Jim. Is it possible that an unjust God rules the universe? No way! He sees all injustice and punishes it accordingly. Sometimes He punishes stubborn people by giving them the kinds of rulers they deserve.

"Why not repent of your ranting against God, Jim? Repent of your foolishness. Stop berating God!

"Do you think it really matters to God how righteous or how sinful you are? It doesn't really touch Him; it touches only people. People don't turn to Him, so He doesn't hear their cries. Jim claims God doesn't see him because God hasn't struck him down for his haughty words. Instead, he ought to be humbling himself before God.

"I think I can teach you guys a few things. God does not let the wicked prosper. He helps the poor and suffering. Even presidents and prime ministers end up in prison if they get too haughty. If they'd listened to God, they would have been OK. Those who don't listen die all shriveled up and worn out. He rescues those who are suffering, but He also uses suffering as a way to teach people. Don't always be expecting a comfortable life—it all too often leads people astray.

(Thunder begins to be heard in the distance.)

"God is so great! He comes with thunder and lightning, driving everyone indoors to get out of the storm, so listen to Him. Jim, you don't understand God or what He does in nature. He is beyond our understanding. He does do justice. So we need to honor Him and look to Him."

Chapter 38

NARRATOR:

Even as Eddy spoke, a storm had been brewing on the horizon, and now it broke in full force, and Jim heard God speaking out of the storm.

GOD:

"So Jim, you think you're pretty smart, do you? Well, I've got a few questions for you. Stand up and see how well you do on my little quiz.

"Where were you when I created the world? How did I form it in just the right size and put it just close enough to the sun that it would support life? How about the ocean? Did you watch

> "WHO CREATES THE WEATHER— THE SNOW, THE RAIN, THE THUNDERSTORM, THE DEW?"

Me make it and set up the beach at Malibu? Say, how about this: Have you ever made the sun come up in the morning? Have you been to the bottom of the ocean? Have you ever seen the gates of death? *Hmmm.* I wonder if you could tell Me where light comes from—or darkness for that matter. You probably have all the answers, don't you? Who creates the weather—the snow, the rain, the thunderstorm, the dew? Are you able to touch the stars in heaven? Do you tell the constellations where to go? Can you take care of the needs of lions or ravens? What about the mountain goats? There are many animals you can't control, but I can. I made the ostrich a fool, but I made horses fantastic, powerful beasts. Are you able to capture the wild beasts that I made?

"Who are you to argue with Me?"

JIM:

"What can I say? I'm too small to speak in Your presence. I've already said enough."

GOD:

"I've got some more questions for you. How dare you question My justice or try to make yourself out to be right and Me wrong? Are you as strong as I am? Can you thunder like I can? Humble a few proud men for me, OK? Then I'll acknowledge your power.

"Think, for a moment, about the power in a single atom. Now, you may think that you've harnessed the power of the atom because you have some stock in the power company. But can you hold an H-bomb in your hand and stop it from exploding? Would you dare approach the core of a nuclear reactor? The power of these things is too awesome for you to understand, yet I am the One who made them all."

JIM:

"I've been a fool to question you. I had only heard of You, but now that I've encountered You face-to-face, I give up. I will not question Your ways ever again!"

NARRATOR:

When the Lord finished speaking to Job, He had a message for Pastor Elwin:

GOD:

"I'm angry with you and your two friends. You haven't spoken right about Me as Jim did. You need to repent and ask Jim to pray for you."

NARRATOR:

Jim's friends did as God had instructed, and Jim prayed for them. Then God began to bless Jim again, and he ended up twice as rich and blessed as he had been in the first place. His stock portfolio blossomed once again, his wife bore him ten more children, and his three daughters were the most beautiful in the entire state of California. Jim lived long and prospered, with the blessing of the Lord.

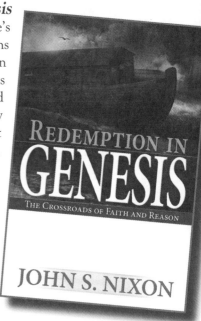